RICHARD ATTENBOROUGH
A Pictorial Film Biography

RICHARD ATTENBOROUGH
A Pictorial Film Biography

David Castell

THE BODLEY HEAD
LONDON SYDNEY
TORONTO

British Library Cataloguing
In Publication Data
Castell, David
Richard Attenborough
A Pictorial Film Biography
I. Title
791.43'092'4   PN1998.A3A

ISBN 0 370 309863 (hardback)
0 370 309898 (paperback)

Introduction © David Castell 1984
Printed in Great Britain for
The Bodley Head Ltd,
9 Bow Street, London WC2E 7AL
by William Clowes Ltd.
Set in Linotron Sabon
by Wyvern Typesetting Ltd.
First published in 1984

Acknowledgements

Acknowledgements and gratitude are due to all the stills cameramen and cartoonists whose work appears in this book and also to the film critics whose reviews are quoted. A number of photographs were kindly provided by the British Film Institute Library with the assistance of Jenny Sussex and, in one particularly elusive instance, by Roger Holman of the National Film Archive.

Introduction

As Hercules in Ben Levy's The Rape of the Belt *in 1956; the last occasion he played on the West End stage.*

As a producer-director-actor, Sir Richard Attenborough occupies a position that is unique in British cinema. He has been working steadily towards it during the quarter century that he has been in film production. During those rich but sometimes difficult years he has ploughed his experience back into the British film industry in the most practical of ways.

In the 1940s he had started to build with a young actor's intuition and appetite upon popular performances in films like *In Which We Serve* and *Brighton Rock*. Everything was against him, not just his perennially boyish looks and the stigma of typecasting, but the belt-and-braces attitudes of an industry that inevitably served yesterday's left-overs as the new *plat du jour*. Gourmands like Attenborough had three choices: to give up, go away or work out a new menu. Several actors found the only tolerable solution to move and work overseas; Attenborough remained to fight within the British system.

He spent the first seventeen years of his forty-year career as an actor, and it is in those years that his success as both producer and director is rooted. Today he is prepared to call himself a director who used to act, just as once he thought of himself as a screen actor who used to work in the theatre. But it was when he crossed behind the cameras that he was able to call on his skills as a compulsive communicator, to put across an understanding of the problems that beset the actors in British films and to suggest how the symptoms and the ailment itself might best be treated.

Nobody who works in the film industry or the related media can go long without encountering Richard Attenborough—he was knighted in 1976. My own first meeting with him was one Saturday night thirteen years ago in the stalls of the now revamped Essoldo cinema in Chelsea.

At the Essoldo cinema in 1970 with (left) John Williams and partner David Castell, PRO John Gregory, a member of the audience and Jock McGregor.

For the exact date, 31 January 1970, I had only to check in a back issue of a programme guide, *Films in London*, that I had launched with my partner John Williams five months previously. We were there that evening to attend one of what the Essoldo publicists could not be dissuaded from calling their 'chat-ins' with the famous. Attenborough's first film as director, *Oh! What a Lovely War*, had opened successfully in the West End towards the end of the previous year and was now leaking out into that precarious area of British film exhibition known as the general release.

This is the hurdle at which many a film falls that has streaked out of the starting gate with the odds stacked in its favour. But Attenborough was sage enough to recognise the danger point in the commercial life of his picture and to throw the weight of his celebrity behind the championing of it by the independent Essoldo circuit.

The final evening performance of *Oh! What a Lovely War* drew to a close with that close-up of five white memorial crosses. Then the camera swings up, out and away to reveal an unimaginably huge vista of crosses, martialled on a sward of downs, a graphic and haunting representation of the scale of lost life in World War I. It is a scene that has the power to move me to tears. The auditorium was kept in tactful darkness for a full minute before the 'chat-in' commenced.

Attenborough piloted an adroit course through the questions of an appreciative, but not obsequiously uncritical audience. When that audience started to drift away in search of last trains, he came down from the stage into the auditorium, greeting old friends and making new ones. He could, and still can, talk the hind leg off a donkey; that night he was like some highly energised reveller anxious to see the party continue.

I learned the technique by which the closing scene of *Oh! What a Lovely War* had been achieved—a still of the first five crosses had been superimposed over the viewfinder of a helicopter-borne camera, the craft then hovering until a perfect marriage of images was attained; they went to 27 takes and used the nineteenth. I learned that it was indeed true that he had sung and danced his way through the score in order to persuade a doubtful mogul to finance the project. I learned that one irate New Yorker had insisted that the entire entertainment was a subversive, veiled metaphor, specifically designed to embarrass 'our President'.

But, best of all, I learned that Attenborough had read and remembered a capsule review of his film in the very first issue of our magazine. I find that we had labelled it, 'An unqualified triumph . . . Joan Littlewood's stage production of World War I translated into pure cinema; an eloquent, angry obituary for a lost generation.' I still stand by those sentiments, but my strongest emotion that January night was delight that someone had actually *read* a magazine that was experiencing great difficulty even in reaching the bookstalls.

Attenborough's enquiries about the progress of the publication, the willingness or reluctance of distribution companies to support it with the advertising that is an essential lifeline; the logistical problems of distribution of the paper itself; these went well beyond polite courtesy. His greeting of a new and minor venture with a generous, informed enthusiasm is typical of the man. I have

With camera operator, Ronnie Taylor, (who, with Billy Williams some years later, was to photograph Gandhi) *lining up a shot for* Oh! What A Lovely War. *From left to right are sound recordist, Simon Kaye, sound maintenance engineer, Desmond Edwards, first assistant, the late Claude Watson and continuity girl, Ann Skinner, who is now a producer in her own right.*

subsequently seen him beam those energies on people and projects within and outside the arts. That particular evening it was an elating validation of a hazardous and foolhardy enterprise. I was half way home in a taxi when I realised with a physical blush that we had not spoken one word about *Oh! What a Lovely War*, nor his career.

Any fundamental journalistic probing would have revealed that at that time his plans to stage a film biography of Mohandas K. Gandhi had already been spun, moth-eaten with setbacks and freshly retexturised. His friend John Mills had chivvied him into directing *Oh! What a Lovely War*. Mills and Len Deighton had worked together on a film treatment, and wanted as a director, 'either someone who knows everything about film-making or someone who knows nothing'. In judging their selection to fall into the latter category, they undersold Attenborough and the production experience of the preceding ten years. Once his debut film was completed, the director clung to it with a terrier-like tenacity and promoted it with every ounce of his considerable energy.

In so doing he was unconsciously rehearsing for the twenty-year decathlon that culminated on the stage of the Dorothy Chandler Pavilion in Los Angeles in April 1983 when the film of *Gandhi* garnered eight of the American Academy of Motion Picture Arts and Sciences' statuettes, known by the most potent and evocative nickname in all cinema: Oscars. No British film has won as many in the entire history of the American Academy.

He was also developing the style of his most personal films as director—*Oh! What a Lovely War* itself, *Young Winston*, *A Bridge Too Far* and, of course, *Gandhi*—a style that either stimulates or offends. Attenborough's concern as a director is with the impact of modern history upon the people who live in the shadow of

Celebrating the Gandhi *Oscars in Hollywood with, left to right, art director, Bob Laing, production designer, Stuart Craig, director of photography, Billy Williams, screenwriter, John Briley, Ben Kingsley, editor, John Bloom and costume designer Bhanu Athaiya. Absent winners are joint director of photography, Ronnie Taylor, British costume designer John Mollo and set dresser, Michael Sierton. A total of thirteen statuettes were presented to crew members who worked within the eight categories for which* Gandhi *was voted best film.*

momentous decisions and events. His tendency is to observe the small comings and goings, the quiet acts of courage performed by ordinary people in an extraordinary arena. But those accounts are selective and revisionist. Built into the films is often a harsh criticism of British attitudes and policies, particularly in military matters, and this anti-Establishment tone frequently angers audiences drawn to the film by Attenborough's background, reputation and public profile.

The anti-war stance permeates each of his four major films as director and they have raised the ire of the militarists in varying degrees. In fact the view of the British in India afforded by *Gandhi* earned more column inches in the correspondence columns of the British national newspapers than any film in living memory. But Attenborough's commitment to entertainment that is not wholly escapist, but has a degree of social comment, has often steered him into squally controversies. There was an initial boycott of *The Angry Silence*, his first film as producer, by the South Wales miners' union. His performance as the mass murderer John Reginald Christie in *10 Rillington Place* was a trigger in a timely debate about the restoration of capital punishment in Britain. The announcement that he would attend the première of *Gandhi* in South Africa also caused a furore, although Attenborough reversed this once screenings had been guaranteed in that country for white, coloured *and* black audiences.

The attitudes that shaped Attenborough's professional career were laid down in the cradle. Born in 1923, he was the eldest of the three sons of Frederick Attenborough MA, Principal of University College, Leicester, and his wife, Mary, and he enjoyed with his brothers David, the broadcaster and traveller, and John a childhood that was comfortable and secure. But, as children of parents who had been ardent supporters of the Labour Party almost since its inception, it was a privilege they were not allowed to take for granted. His parents evidently exercised in their daily life a practical idealism and muscular Christianity that worked by example.

As Pro-Chancellor of Sussex University, Attenborough participated in the 1978 ceremony bestowing an honorary degree on his brother, David.

With fellow actor Campbell Copelin, director, John Boulting, and his parents who came to watch the filming of Brighton Rock.

He was waylaid by the theatre while still a young teenager, first appearing on the school stage as a fairy in *Iolanthe*. With the tacit approval and encouragement of his mother, who was president of the Leicester Little Theatre, an amateur company of exceptionally high standing, he set his heart on a career in the performing arts.

In the light of failing scholastic achievements, his father set an ultimatum. Richard could apply for the Leverhulme Scholarship at RADA—the Royal Academy of Dramatic Art, of which he has been chairman since 1970—but, if that failed, as seemed the more likely outcome of the audition, he must apply himself with renewed vigour to academic work. Happily he won the scholarship and went to London to train to become an actor at the age of seventeen, a turning point that was acknowledged by his father with a mixture of pride and resignation.

It was while he was still studying at RADA that Attenborough won his first film role, that of the young stoker who deserts his post aboard a torpedoed destroyer in *In Which We Serve*. The film's writer and co-director Noël Coward had deployed scouts to find unfamiliar faces to play the young sailors in the film, but it was the eminent agent, Al Parker, who proposed Attenborough to Coward. One of Parker's clients was the actress Peggy Cummins, who had appeared with Attenborough in Eugene O'Neill's play *Ah! Wilderness* at Palmers Green. Parker attended a performance and communicated his enthusiasm about the young actor to Coward.

In Which We Serve was based on Lord Louis Mountbatten's early wartime experiences and most of the shooting was done on a mock-up of his ship in a tank at Denham Studios. One of the stream of visitors who came to see the lifelike model was Lord Louis himself. Coward chanced to introduce Attenborough to the man who was later to become a powerful ally in the setting up of *Gandhi*.

As an essay in wartime propaganda, the portrait of shipboard life given by *In Which We Serve* is without peer. Coward won an Oscar nomination for his script and the film itself was nominated as Best Picture. Its proud patriotism was Coward's own and it was to be the most confidently realised of the films with which he was involved. For Attenborough it was the most fortunate of breaks, although his striking debut performance was one that caused him to be typecast for many years.

Still at RADA, Attenborough met his fellow student Sheila Sim, and they married in 1945. For the fifteen years before her retirement from the screen after the birth of their third child their careers ran along parallel and occasionally converging lines. In Roy Boulting's production *The Guinea Pig* Attenborough, then twenty-six, was still able to convince as a schoolboy, a tobacconist's son who wins a scholarship to a public school and there encounters curt snobbery and the wrong kind of lessons in class. Ironically Sheila Sim played her husband's housemistress!

The baby-round face that cursed his early acting career was already taking its toll even though, the previous year, he had been cast compellingly against type in *Brighton Rock*. Graham Greene, who in his novel had created the character of the psychopathic Pinkie Brown, felt that Attenborough might lack the necessary aura of evil for the film, even though Greene had approved the actor's stage performance. But his portrait of the ice-blooded razor thug took on even more frightening life on the screen. For a generation who had grown up on baby-faced killers by the score in American gangster movies, here was one that withstood psychological examination and was thought out in the tiniest detail. Greene himself was completely won over and wrote to correct his initial misjudgment. But for Attenborough the part was not, as it had promised to be, a signpost to better roles.

Although he has been courted by Hollywood studios, Attenborough only once signed a long-term contract. That was with the Boulting brothers, a major film-making force in the Britain of the Forties and Fifties. Attenborough had met them when he was seconded from the RAF Flying Training Command to the Royal Air Force Film Unit to appear in the 1944 production *Journey Together* with Edward G. Robinson. By the late Fifties the Boultings had embarked upon a series of gently mocking social satires that were resoundingly popular with British audiences. After endless reprises, all of them inferior, of naval ratings in the manner of *In Which We Serve* or snivelling psychopaths *à la Brighton Rock*, the Boultings offered a hand of rescue in the vortex of Attenborough's career. Their three comedies, *Private's Progress*, *Brothers in Law* and *I'm All Right Jack* restored the actor's confidence and credibility but, by the time the last of these was released in 1959, Attenborough had elected to hijack his own career in a move that was to have a lasting effect.

The British cinema of the Fifties had been desperately parochial. The staple diet was light comedy, thrillers and war films. If a producer with a more adventurous idea succeeded in getting his film before the cameras, he would almost certainly find himself stonewalled when he delivered his picture into the hands of

With his wife, Sheila, at the time they appeared together in The Guinea Pig.

The twin Boulting brothers, John (left) and Roy.

apathetic distributors who knew all too well the 'mixture as before' policy prescribed by the two major circuits, a duopoly that had a stranglehold on the creative growth of an indigenous British cinema.

In America, where the contractual hold of the studios posed a threat to the actor equal to that of the British distribution and exhibition bottleneck, some of the major stars, Burt Lancaster and Kirk Douglas among them, had started to set up production companies of their own, in order to manage their careers and protect their professional interests. The odds against a similar scheme succeeding in Britain were all the greater, yet Attenborough and his career-long friend Bryan Forbes decided that this would be the way in which to express and demonstrate their appetite for a better British cinema. They formed Beaver Films.

The theme of trade unionism, lightly guyed in *I'm All Right Jack*, was treated in earnest in Beaver's debut production, *The Angry Silence*. It was an almost wilfully difficult picture to tackle as a first project, the story of a factory worker who, for his refusal to join an unofficial strike, is intimidated and later sent to Coventry by his workmates. It would have been so much easier for Attenborough and Forbes to have compromised, to have tested the production waters with a cautious toe, perhaps attempting another of those mild but honourable comedies at which each man had already proved himself adept. But it was because the British cinema of the Fifties succumbed almost permanently to that kind of compromise that the friends had felt a need to rebel against the movie chores they were being given and to make their idiosyncratic stand. So *The Angry Silence* it was to be; Forbes to script, Attenborough to produce and star as the victimised hero.

Beaver flew the standard of an indigenous cinema, pictures that were rooted in British life and British manners. The films they made were socially aware and responsible works, but *The Angry Silence* was the most politically engaged. The experienced Guy Green was set to direct—he, Attenborough and Pier Angeli, who played Attenborough's wife, had discussed their plans to work together on

With Bryan Forbes and Pier Angeli during the making of The Angry Silence.

13

this subject during the location shooting of the previous year's rather dire *SOS Pacific*. But the new package did not arouse the enthusiasm of backers who were all too happy with the return on investment guaranteed by films about hapless medical students and vintage motor-cars.

Finally Attenborough's old mentors, the Boultings, piloted the project into the safe harbour of British Lion, though their maximum agreed investment necessitated further scything cuts in an already pared budget. Thus it was the idea dawned of the principals taking only a nominal payment with the balance deferred in the form of a percentage of the film's ultimate profitability. Today that kind of financial juggling has become debased and is often a smokescreen for a bankruptcy of ideas as well as money, but in the Britain of 1959 it was a startling pledge of faith in the character and future of Beaver.

If the delirious reception by the reviewers had been reflected at the box-office, *The Angry Silence* would have gone quickly into profit. As it was, it turned out to be a slow but steady earner—all the investors got their money back and a profit on their stake—while the industry looked with interest to see if Beaver could build on this *succès d'éstime*.

Attenborough and Forbes joined forces next with Michael Relph and Basil Dearden, Jack Hawkins and Guy Green in a consortium called Allied Film Makers and it was under this banner that they made *The League of Gentlemen*, a wry comedy in the Ealing

Filming Whistle Down the Wind *in Lancashire. The spectators and unit on the hillside include, left to right, camera operator, David Harcourt, editor Max Benedict, Mary Hayley Bell, John Mills, Hayley Mills and continuity girl, Penny Daniels.*

tradition, written by Forbes. Jack Hawkins played a former army officer planning a bank raid along military lines. Attenborough headed the platoon of conscripts to Hawkins's nefarious army. It was particularly apt that this comedy about neglected talent and energy being harnessed for use against the Establishment that has ignored it was the first collaboration of Attenborough and Forbes after the debut of Beaver—their own league of gentlemen.

They returned to Beaver for *Whistle Down the Wind*, but whereas *The Angry Silence* had showcased Attenborough as producer-star, now the seesaw tilted in Forbes's favour with Attenborough himself invisible to the public in the solo role of producer. The film was to star Hayley Mills, then at the zenith of her success as a Disney child star, as the eldest of three children of a Lancashire widower. Deprived of much family attention, they inhabit a world of their own making and, when they stumble on a stranger sheltering in a barn on their father's farm, they take his surprised cry of, 'Jesus Christ!' as one of identification. The man is a hunted murderer and acts of worship and betrayal follow before the children see their hero being frisked by the arresting police officers, his arms outstretched as though in a pose of crucifixion.

Whistle Down the Wind, which launched Alan Bates's film career, was based on the story by Mary Hayley Bell (mother of Hayley Mills and wife of John) and scripted by Keith Waterhouse and Willis Hall. The original director was to have been Guy Green, with Forbes and Attenborough to co-produce. But Green dropped out and, after some hasty pleading by Attenborough at the eleventh hour, Forbes was given his debut directorial assignment.

The film once more garnered praise for Beaver, their standards and endeavour. Bryan Forbes's directing career was proudly launched and he stayed on as both writer *and* director of the remaining two films that Attenborough was to produce in this period. *The L-Shaped Room* was taken from a Lynne Reid Banks novel about London's bedsitter-land. Leslie Caron was the lonely heroine with an unwanted pregnancy, Tom Bell the aspiring writer who transforms everything he sees and experiences into material for his stories. *Seance on a Wet Afternoon* was to be their final collaboration and it was perhaps the most skilfully realised of the Beaver films. It also won for Attenborough the Best Actor award of the Society of Film and Television Arts (later renamed the British Academy of Film and Television Arts).

Before *Seance on a Wet Afternoon*, Attenborough had acted in *The Dock Brief*, a legal shaggy dog story by John Mortimer that gave him the chance to pit his talent for comedy against that of the awesome Peter Sellers, then at the peak of his popularity. It is the story of an incompetent barrister (Sellers) who imagines his reputation being belatedly made by his defence of Attenborough's mild, seedy, self-confessed murderer. Their tolerance of one another's shortcomings and their mutual support is as touching as it is funny, but the prison cell rehearsal for the court appearance— with Attenborough required to play not only the accused, but judge, jury and all the other necessary parts—is a dazzling piece of sustained bravura that ensured that for once Sellers did not scoop all the attention or the notices.

As Attenborough entered his forties, the round face became a positive curse. Consequently he allowed his screen self to retreat

With Audrey Hepburn, when they were voted Best Actress and Best Actor of 1964 by the Society of Film and Television Arts.

into a series of make-ups and disguises. *The Dock Brief* had found him dowdy and downcast; *Guns at Batasi* was to see him transformed into a bristling Regimental Sergeant Major; *10 Rillington Place* would show him converted into the true-life figure of mass murderer John Reginald Christie.

But this preoccupation with disguise began in *Seance on a Wet Afternoon*. As Billy, the asthmatic, lovelorn and dangerously adoring husband of a fake spiritualist (Kim Stanley), he was barely recognisable—thinning hair slicked sideways, a boxer-flat nose and a sad moustache making a strangulated assertion of hen-pecked masculinity. It was as though the years of emotional abuse and battering by his self-deluding wife had had a physical effect on Billy. He is drawn, against his weak will, into her scheme to kidnap the daughter of a rich industrialist, demand and collect a ransom; then she will volunteer her psychic services to 'divine' the whereabouts of the missing child and therefore bask in the resulting publicity. The perfectly modulated performances of the two stars ensured that Beaver's swansong was one to be remembered. Kim Stanley won an Oscar nomination for her role and did not appear on the screen again until she played the mother of Frances Farmer in the 1982 film *Frances*, again winning an Oscar nomination.

The demise of Beaver was amicable. Forbes wanted to go to Hollywood (to make *King Rat*); Attenborough did not. The Beaver films were modest successes in commercial terms, but their example was powerful. They showed that artists of calibre and courage *could* pilot a course through production, distribution and exhibition and find an audience that was responsive to and appreciative of intelligent British films. Many years later, talking about the role within the media of Britain's fourth television channel (of which he is Deputy Chairman), Attenborough was to say that this was 'to achieve a position in which we can allow our creative artists to fail'. Beaver was just such a laboratory, though the luxury of failure was one they could hardly have afforded.

By the time *Seance on a Wet Afternoon* was delivered for distribution, Attenborough was already caught in the tentacles of a production that was fated almost to outrun *The Mousetrap*, the 1951 Agatha Christie stage thriller in whose original cast he had co-starred with his wife Sheila. 'I think we might get a nice little run out of it,' the author had said on the first night of the pre-London

Prime Minister James Callaghan was the guest of honour in 1977 at a lunch to celebrate the 25th anniversary of The Mousetrap's *West End first night.*

Motilal Kothari acts as guide to Lord Louis Mountbatten at the 1969 centenary exhibition of Gandhi memorabilia which he mounted at Congress House in London.

Receiving the Padma Bhushan from President Zail Singh at the 1983 investiture in New Delhi.

tour. The play is still running in the West End of London today.

If the departure of Forbes to America left space in Attenborough's working life, it was soon to be swamped by the project that consumed twenty years of his life. *Gandhi*. The gestation period here was so huge and Attenborough's commitment to it so tenacious that there were those around him who began to fear for the continuing validity of his professional judgment. *Gandhi* permeated every crevice of his life, and the way in which he withstood a legion of setbacks, disappointments and collapses of the project was awesome.

There is a full and colourful account of Attenborough's consuming obsession in his own book, *In Search of Gandhi* (The Bodley Head, 1982) and a brief chronology of the key events must suffice here. The seed of the *Gandhi* project had been sown by Motilal Kothari who made contact with Attenborough in 1962. Kothari had been a devout follower of Mohandas K. Gandhi, the Mahatma or 'Great Soul' of India. After Gandhi's assassination in 1948, Kothari found life in India too painful and he came to London with his wife, an English schoolteacher, and worked at the Indian High Commission. His discipleship took the form of enthusing others to communicate Gandhi's pacifist and humanitarian principles. In the case of Richard Attenborough, the instrument of this enthusiasm was to be Louis Fischer's biography, *The Life of Mahatma Gandhi* (Jonathan Cape, 1951). Kothari gave Attenborough a copy in the quiet, mystical certainty that it would woo him round to a position of agreeing to try and set up a film biography.

Attenborough was indeed seduced by the account of Gandhi's life and teachings — the single sentence that hooked him was Gandhi's statement, 'It has always been a mystery to me how men can feel themselves honoured by the humiliation of their fellow beings.' He set about the daunting task of trying to raise the necessarily large budget. The modest successes of Beaver had been achieved on minimal investments; now Attenborough was asking a prince's ransom. Everyone could see the hazards attendant upon a large-budget, long-schedule production to be made on location in India. Nobody could see the commercial magnetism in the story of the man Winston Churchill once called 'a half-naked seditious fakir'.

It was Lord Louis Mountbatten who effected Attenborough's introduction to Pandit Nehru and his daughter Indira Gandhi, who was much later to follow in her father's footsteps as Prime Minister of India. Permissions were sought, formal blessings given in the Indian Parliament, scripts drafted and re-written.

But, with the death in May 1964 of Nehru, the project's foremost and powerful champion within India, *Gandhi* suffered the first of a series of collapses.

The British Academy Best Actor award was Attenborough's a second time for the performance in *Guns at Batasi*, a modest adventure dealing with political upheavals in a newly independent African state. Central to the film is Attenborough's ultimate character part, a bellowing, ramrod-straight Regimental Sergeant Major who dominates the picture as masterfully as the character commands his men. Attenborough evidently relished the opportunity to tackle a character so remote from himself and spent five weeks at Chelsea Barracks watching RSMs on the parade ground and meeting them in the Mess. That investment of time and preparation paid off handsomely in the best set of reviews Attenborough had received.

He had long resisted the idea of going to Hollywood but had enjoyed the experience of working in John Sturges's prisoner-of-war adventure *The Great Escape*, based on Paul Brickhill's account of an actual mass exodus from a German camp. For the first time Attenborough was part of a truly international company; Steve McQueen, James Garner, James Coburn and Charles Bronson were among his co-stars. The film, a solid and enduring box-office success, had been made in West Germany, but the term 'Hollywood' carries its own inverted commas with it and is no respecter of actual geography. So pleasing had been his first taste of international film-making that Attenborough now agreed to film in Hollywood.

There he made three films for 20th Century-Fox. The first was *The Flight of the Phoenix*, best in the then-burgeoning genre of desert survival movies. James Stewart played the guilt-ridden pilot of a 'plane downed in the desert, Attenborough the nervy, booze-dependent navigator who shares a responsibility for the crash. Among the co-stars was Peter Finch whom he had approached, as he had Albert Finney, Tom Courtenay, Alec Guinness and Dirk Bogarde, to play Gandhi. All had declined.

In the unlikely setting of Yuma, Arizona, during location filming for The Flight of the Phoenix *James Stewart throws a party to celebrate the Queen's birthday and invites the entire British contingent. With Attenborough and Stewart here are Ian Bannen (left) and Peter Finch.*

His second 'Hollywood' film was *The Sand Pebbles*, a sprawling shipboard epic about the American involvement in the Chinese civil war of 1926, and a picture that reunited him with his co-star of *The Great Escape*, Steve McQueen. His final Hollywood act was to give an extraordinary and uncharacteristic demonstration of his gifts as a song-and-dance man in the otherwise lacklustre musical *Dr Dolittle*, based on the children's stories by Hugh Lofting. Attenborough was a last-minute replacement for an actor who was found incapable of just those musical talents for which he had been hired and, as a fairground showman, Attenborough performed the number 'I've Never Seen Anything Like It in My Life' about a two-headed llama. His evident joy and considerable energy made the number the highspot of the film and won him the second of his six Golden Globe awards.

Beginning to think that the reluctance of backers to finance *Gandhi*, and that of major actors to appear in it, might have something to do with his complete inexperience as a director, Attenborough decided to direct another film by way of rehearsal. He considered but declined a directing assignment while still in Hollywood and returned to Britain to receive a telephone call from his old friend and colleague John Mills. Mills and Len Deighton believed that they had cracked the problem of how to adapt Joan Littlewood's stage hit *Oh! What a Lovely War* for the cinema.

Attenborough's initial resistance to the project evaporated when he read the script. In the production at the Theatre Royal, Stratford East, the war had been presented as a Brechtian entertainment by a pierrot company; in Len Deighton's screen treatment the main scenes were to be staged within the amusements of Brighton Pier—from whose balustrades Pinkie Brown had fallen to his watery death at the end of *Brighton Rock*—with some of the musical numbers spilling out on to the Sussex Downs. There is an end-of-pier recruitment show; soldiers leave for the war on miniature, narrow-gauge trains; military conferences take place in glass-roofed pavilions; the death toll in the Battle of the Somme is displayed on a cricket scoreboard while Field-Marshal Sir Douglas Haig (John Mills) conducts proceedings from the top of a pier helter-skelter.

The use of songs throughout is ironic and it is unsurprising that Paramount, who backed the film, could not easily envisage from a bald synopsis the kind of picture that might be delivered to them. It was at this juncture, primed no doubt by his experiences on *Dr Dolittle*, that Attenborough sang and danced his way through the score to win the endorsement of Paramount's boss, the late Charles Bludhorn. It must have been a persuasive audition because, at the end of it, he left the building with a commitment that was as good as Paramount's cheque for six million dollars. The only rider was that he had to secure the services of six international stars. Attenborough netted thirteen deserving of that description and Laurence Olivier's statement that he was prepared to work for the basic minimum daily rate was an example that most of the distinguished cast were delighted to follow.

In directing terms, Mills had had the right instinct about Attenborough, not merely in that he could find the fire and the passion for the production, but also in that he would have a clear telescope view of what he wanted to achieve, uncluttered by any

foreknowledge of the difficulties. That closing image of the infinity of white crosses on the Downs, while a soldiers' pastiche of Jerome Kern's 'They Wouldn't Believe Me' swells up on the soundtrack, was just one example of Attenborough refusing to accept on the screen an image that did not coincide with the one already in his mind's eye.

Although he maintains that, as an actor, he is a director of actors, that actors are his primary conductors of thought and emotion, Attenborough has gained a considerable technical knowledge through his four large-scale films. His sympathetic handling has certainly helped guide other players to performances that test and stretch them—the comparatively untried Simon Ward in *Young Winston*, the towering central performance in *Gandhi* of Ben Kingsley, then quite inexperienced in the trying stop-go techniques of film-making—but his detailed preparation in research and a questing examination of camerawork and editing have sprung several surprises.

When *Oh! What a Lovely War* opened to critical acclaim, the resistance to the idea of Attenborough directing *Gandhi* began perceptibly to melt. But in the years that he had been forced by the necessity of earning a living to set the project aside, Motilal Kothari had grown restless. He had sought Attenborough's permission to attempt to mount a production elsewhere and director David Lean and his regular writer Robert Bolt were now toying with the idea. In a rather bizarre move, they even asked Attenborough if he would consider playing the Mahatma himself. Attenborough is honest enough to admit that he hesitated a full minute before declining.

Directing a front line trench scene for Oh! What a Lovely War *on the municipal refuse tip at Brighton.*

Directing Simon Ward in Young Winston.

After all, the idea of himself as Gandhi was no more extraordinary than that of some other actors whose names were bandied about in those years, while among those still to be mooted were Dustin Hoffman, Robert de Niro and Marlon Brando!

What was not melting, however, was the resistance to the idea as a commercially viable production. Lean and Bolt might have got the picture off the ground, but first they had 'a little film' to make. That was *Ryan's Daughter*, which expanded to fill three working years. In that interim Kothari and Louis Fischer died, coincidentally on the same day in 1971.

Before going on to direct his second picture, *Young Winston*, Attenborough paused to act in *10 Rillington Place*, the horrific tale of Timothy Evans (John Hurt), wrongly executed for a murder committed by his landlord, John Reginald Christie. It was a celebrated miscarriage of British justice and, despite the revulsion Attenborough felt for the character of Christie and the difficulties he experienced in playing the man, the moment was exactly right to point out through such a film the fallibility of any jury that is given the power to take a man's life. Christie was himself executed before capital punishment was abolished in Britain in 1965 but only five years later, when *10 Rillington Place* went before the cameras, there was a mounting pressure for its restoration.

Young Winston, based on Churchill's *My Early Years*, was devised as 'an intimate epic', and so it was; intimate in its examination of family minutiae that helped forge the budding character, epic in its scenes of battle and adventure. The film took the statesman from childhood to the age of 26, when he made his first major speech in the House of Commons, an attack on military expenditure and the arms race within Europe. The speech was also a vindication of his father, Lord Randolph Churchill, who had fallen from grace in the eyes of the Tory Party for his own implacable opposition to military spending. The scenes that spoke most eloquently were those that examined the character of Winston in the light of what he was later to become and to represent. The film was neither a pedantically detailed biography nor a jingoistic epic, but an imaginative investigation of the boy who was to become one of the most famous men of his century.

'What's to become of you?' The question of Robert Shaw's despairing Lord Randolph to his dunce of a son rings through Carl Foreman's script. The need to be noticed, to collect medals, to succeed in politics: all seem to stem from the thwarted desire for paternal approval.

The form was that of a mosaic, the chronology fractured so that one leapt about in time, from maturity back to childhood and, in a rather touching coda, forward to a vision of the aged Churchill dozing in his Chartwell study and dreaming that he is visited by Lord Randolph. The father looks incredulously at the canvases in the study and asks his son a little despairingly, 'Is this what you *do*?' not realising that this is only a spare-time relaxation and that Winston has followed him into political life and achieved the highest office in the land. One wonders what Attenborough's own father might make now of his son's career choice.

Despite the fact that much of the film was shot in Morocco (with Wales doubling for Natal), *Young Winston* captures elegantly the dying fall of the Empire. The examination of the central characters,

Winston (Simon Ward), Lord Randolph and Jennie Jerome (Anne Bancroft), was made more penetrating by an anachronistic but curiously satisfying device of having each grilled probingly by an off-screen interviewer, as though for an aggressive contemporary television programme.

With *Young Winston* there crystallised Attenborough's singular gift for examining the impact of recent history upon the people who live in its wake. It was to be another four years before he directed again and of the films in which he acted during the interim, two were of note. He gave a sound performance in Michael Anderson's craftsmanlike film of the play *Conduct Unbecoming,* and played opposite the legendary John Wayne in a London-set police thriller, *Brannigan.* Wayne played the cop from across the water, in England to extradite a Chicago gangster and requiring the assistance of Attenborough's dapper Commander Swann of Scotland Yard.

In his continuing search for backers of the Gandhi film, Attenborough had previously met the Hollywood producer Joseph E. Levine, who had expressed an interest in the project. Nothing had come to fruition with Levine so *Gandhi* had passed to Warner Brothers who were committed to start shooting. Levine, a seasoned veteran of the industry, planned to produce a screen version of Cornelius Ryan's *A Bridge Too Far* and invited Attenborough to direct. Naturally, with *Gandhi* hopefully so imminent, he declined. But Levine caught him on the rebound when, just eight days later,

With the exception of Magic, *John Mills has been a leading player in every film Attenborough has directed and the latter admits that without his friend and colleague of forty years as a member of his cast he is 'uncomfortable'. Here they are pictured on location for* Young Winston.

Mrs Indira Gandhi declared a state of emergency in India and all possibility of scheduled location shooting evaporated.

A Bridge Too Far documented and dramatised the nine days of Operation Market Garden, the bold single thrust aimed at terminating World War II by the winter of 1944. It became a bewildering mixture of battlefield politics, bad luck, worse weather, miscalculation, sheer muddle and raw courage. Attenborough immediately saw it as a savage indictment of war.

There is one scene towards the end of the film in which a posse of high military brass assemble on a balcony, dress-circle observers in the theatre of war watching a play that has taken an unexpected and unpopular turn. As they survey the carnage they have sanctioned, they begin to fidget and to shrug off responsibility. It was the fault of the 'planes, the radios, the weather in England. As the Polish Major General Sosabowski, not one to share the advance high spirits over 'the party at Arnhem', Gene Hackman adds sombrely, 'Whenever anyone says, "Let's play the war game today," everybody dies.' It is the only moment in this three-hour film that Attenborough and his writer, William Goldman, spelled out their anti-war message in words of one syllable. For the rest of the time it was left to the vainglorious muddle of war to condemn itself.

The first of three chapters deals with the hurried planning of the exercise, seen from both sides, with German and Dutch dialogue very properly sub-titled. Here Attenborough's agile cameras and

With producer Joseph E. Levine and screenwriter William Goldman during the making of A Bridge Too Far.

John Addison's stirring score share an optimistic elation that is only nigglingly undermined in the full hour before the first shot is fired. Then *A Bridge Too Far* comes down to earth with a grim newsreel perspective, the fighting savage and confused, as principles and ideals are extinguished in the reality of war.

Finally it becomes a black and bitter tragedy. With a careful division of villainy between the Allies and the enemy, it is the civilians who emerge as the heroes of Arnhem. The most affecting performances are those of Laurence Olivier as Doctor Spaander and Liv Ullman as Kate ter Horst, the Dutch woman who turned her home into a hospital and her garden into a graveyard.

The dazzlingly stellar cast, which also included Dirk Bogarde, James Caan, Michael Caine, Sean Connery, Edward Fox, Elliott Gould, Anthony Hopkins, Hardy Kruger, Ryan O'Neal, Robert Redford and Maximilian Schell, assists the viewer in finding his bearings quickly in a maze so complicated that even those taking part did not always know their whereabouts. 'It took fourteen superstars and a cast of thousands to make this once-in-a-lifetime film!' bragged the publicity line. But whereas the line-up was similar to that which helped *Oh! What a Lovely War* off the ground nine years earlier, notions of deferred payments or of the artists working for the minimum daily rate did not apply here. The practice of stars receiving a percentage had become a commonplace in the years since *The Angry Silence* but, because of the way that Levine had pre-sold the film around the world, it was not possible in this

With the late Geoffrey Unsworth, one of Britain's finest directors of photography, much admired and greatly missed.

Kate ter Horst, the Dutch Second World War heroine, and Liv Ullman who protrayed her in A Bridge Too Far.

instance. The staggering lump sums offered to some of the players attracted much criticism and, when the camera rolled in Deventer in Holland, *A Bridge Too Far* had the largest starting budget of any film made thus far. Once again Attenborough's complex involvement in and responsibility to schedules and budgets would eventually prove invaluable to the making of *Gandhi*.

Attenborough's deal with Levine (who was still muttering about *Gandhi*) also involved the direction of *Magic* in America. But before fulfilling that contractual obligation, he flew to Calcutta to appear as an actor in *The Chess Players* for Satyajit Ray, so honoured by the invitation that he did not ask even to read the script. This was the first film to be made in Hindi (and the first in full colour) by the master Bengali film-maker. It was set in 1856 at the time of the East India Company's annexation of the kingdom of Oudh and it uses the metaphor of a chess game. The obsessive players who appear throughout the film find that even India's national game has been taken over by the British and new rules imposed. Meanwhile General Sir James Outram, the British Resident, demands the abdication of the king. He is the agent of the Governor General, Lord Dalhousie, who alleges corruption and misrule as reasons for taking Oudh from a ruler whose culture and code of conduct the Britons cannot understand. *The Chess Players* presents the conflict as an aggressive example of British imperialism and Attenborough's own excellent performance as Outram, who views the king with staunchly Calvinist distaste, was a stronger and more inherently

With Laurence Olivier, on the set of A Bridge Too Far. *Six years earlier he had asked Attenborough to become his associate director at the National Theatre. The offer was regretfully declined, mainly because it would have meant abandoning any possibility of ever producing and directing* Gandhi.

critical representation of the British presence in India than anything in *Gandhi*, which was subsequently to come under attack for its supposedly anti-British tone.

Magic was an unexpected punctuation mark in the sentence of Attenborough's directing career. It is clearly the odd film out, with very few characters, a small and claustrophobic setting. It was William Goldman's adaptation of his own novel about a homicidally schizophrenic ventriloquist, a plot outline that inevitably invites comparison with the episode in the 1945 Ealing portmanteau film *Dead of Night*, in which Michael Redgrave played outstandingly a ventriloquist haunted by his own dummy. Despite its title, *Magic* eschewed almost all suggestions of the supernatural and honed in on the mental confusion of a man who diverts his emotional energies through a piece of wood. Thus the dummy blurts out, in crude terms, the affection for an old flame (Ann-Margret) that the ventriloquist 'himself' cannot articulate; and when the entertainer's agent (Burgess Meredith) comes to realise the dangerous dereliction of his client's mind, it is the dummy that kills him. Murder by, as well as with, a blunt instrument.

Attenborough had earlier defined the parameters of his film-making interests — 'I have never enjoyed total escapism and I dislike gratuitous violence and that rules out most things; I also enjoy some kind of social content.' He must have approached this fairly brutal thriller with trepidation. Nevertheless he turned in a tense and exciting piece of work that disturbed the small hairs on the back of the neck with its skilful pacing, the slyest of hints at the paranormal and a superb performance by Anthony Hopkins as the deranged central character, yet again marking Attenborough as an actor's director.

Anthony Hopkins was another of the actors seriously in the running to star in *Gandhi*. If ever it happened. Then suddenly it did. It had been so long on the back burner that the interest in the project by a new British production company, Goldcrest, excited few but Attenborough. But they said yes and meant it. They raised two thirds of the $22 million budget from non-industry sources; Attenborough raised the balance from India.

The cameras began to turn in November 1980. The delay had

Displaying the attention to detail that is part of his style as a director by regulating the exact density of autumn leaves blowing past the camera during an atmospheric sequence in Magic.

been fortuitous. Despite the continuing stress factor, Attenborough's enthusiasm had remained undimmed and his technical ability and creative maturity to tackle the film had increased beyond measure in the long hiatus. The awakening worldwide of strong pacifist feelings, a renewed faith in humanitarian principles, firm views among the young against imperialism and colonialism; these exposed a box-office nerve that *Gandhi* was to strike. There had also been a move away from the absolute commercial necessity for star names above the title, a stricture that had circumscribed *Oh! What a Lovely War* and *A Bridge Too Far*; this allowed Ben Kingsley, a stalwart of the Royal Shakespeare Company and half Indian by birth, to play Gandhi as his first major screen role. Finally, John Briley's script, shaped in a huge circular flashback from the

With Jake Eberts, Chief Executive of Goldcrest Films and Television. As a result of their being introduced by screenwriter John Briley, it was Eberts who, in 1980, amassed the greater part of the budget needed to make Gandhi.

Receiving the Martin Luther King 1983 Peace Prize from the civil rights leader's widow, Coretta Scott King, in Atlanta, Georgia.

assassination at the opening back through 56 years of Gandhi's life, recalled the epic British pictures of the Sixties, particularly *Lawrence of Arabia*, now newly revered by audiences too young to have appreciated their narrative clarity when first they appeared.

It is impossible to guess what might have happened if *Gandhi* had slipped effortlessly into production when Motilal Kothari suggested it in the early Sixties. It might have been a decent or indeed a memorable film, but I am certain that it would not then have struck the extraordinary responsive chord that it has with modern audiences. The fate that occasioned all those delays was surely a benign one.

Attenborough believed, with this as with every project, that the film-maker's responsibility to his picture does not end with the final 'Cut!' As its producer, he worked unceasingly to promote the film in the months preceding the premières (Delhi, London, Washington, Toronto, New York, and Los Angeles within a week), all of which he attended. The results were rewarding, a publicity bonanza and reviews that were unstinting in their praise. There was, of course, a dread that the film, after such a long period of gestation, might not match the effort and the energy invested in it but critics were almost unanimous in their acclaim.

Attenborough's confident mastery of narrative technique and the smouldering passion that lies banked within the film were central to the film's success, but he gives due credit to John Briley's spare, literate script that condensed a life and distilled it into a thread of dense, weighty scenes; and to Ben Kingsley's unfaltering performance as Gandhi himself, becoming quite properly invisible in the role in the way that a lesser actor could never have achieved.

RIGHT
With John Briley and Ben Kingsley at the 1983 Hollywood Foreign Press Association's Golden Globe award ceremony.

28

The Vice-President of the British Academy of Film and Television Arts receives its highest accolade, the 1983 Fellowship, from Princess Anne who is the Academy's President.

Steven Spielberg's *E.T.*, trailing a massive reputation and already well on the way to becoming the biggest box-office hit of all time, moved into Leicester Square one week after *Gandhi* but failed to dent the extraordinary commercial performance of Attenborough's film. That pattern was repeated worldwide, even in rural areas where cinema-going was judged to be a lost habit. Spielberg was also backed for a directing Oscar for *E.T.* but, when the Directors' Guild of America gave their award to Attenborough, the Oscar scales tipped towards *Gandhi*. The Guild's awards are the most reliable barometer by which to predict the American Academy voting. 'E.T., phone Gandhi', was how the *Los Angeles Times* headlined the story about the Oscar odds now being offered by bookmakers.

In the event *Gandhi* swept the board, first at the British Academy of Film and Television Arts and then, one month later, at the Oscar ceremony in Los Angeles. Each Academy bestowed its Best Film award, voted Attenborough Best Director and Ben Kingsley Best Actor. The film won five British Academy awards and eight Oscars, consolidating the triumph in America of British cinema. The previous year *Chariots of Fire* had carried off the Best Film statuette. Only once before in the history of the American Academy have British films won two years running: they were *Lawrence of Arabia* and *Tom Jones* in 1962 and 1963 respectively.

The smile of a fickle industry can last for one tuxedo-ed evening, but the success of *Gandhi* has an importance more resonant for a British film industry that is reviving despite government apathy. The British end of the budget had been collected via agencies wholly unaccustomed to film investment, from sources as disparate as the publishers Pearson Longman, the Post Office Superannuation Fund and the National Coal Board's Pension Fund. *Gandhi* remains

Meeting Mother Teresa whilst acting as adviser to a documentary team recording her life and work.

Goldcrest's biggest single investment in a film, and the sight of their flagship steaming into harbour with the certainty of massive profit has subsequently eased the burden of several film-makers.

Attenborough has become Chairman of Goldcrest Films and that position, combined with the chairmanship of the British Film Institute and Deputy-Chairmanship of Channel Four, gives him a powerful voice in the funding, distribution and exhibition of British films. The lesson he learned during his own apprenticeship was that when these vital areas are all in the absolute control of an over-cautious industry, there can be no opportunity for the risk and experiment by which cinema grows and evolves. Only when there are viable alternatives to the hitherto accountant-dominated studio system, to the desperate caution of Wardour Street and to the duopoly of the major circuits can fledgling film-makers have a chance to see their films made, distributed and exhibited. Although *Gandhi* was one of the biggest films of recent years and one of the more traditional in form, its track record and that of its producer-director have helped in a most important way to lay a path for other film-makers.

Attenborough said earlier this year, 'If I had to make a conscious decision now between acting and directing, I would have no problem in deciding that I want to continue to direct.' Already he is preparing with passion and single-mindedness a film about the English revolutionary Tom Paine. But in what he has achieved, both above and below the plimsoll line of that stricken vessel that was once the British film industry, he can claim to have been the senior architect of its rescue.

In counterpoint to that debut performance forty years ago in *In Which We Serve*, Attenborough can now be seen as the stoker who did *not* desert his post.

With Meryl Streep, Ben Kingsley
and the American Academy's four
most prestigious Oscars at the
Dorothy Chandler Pavilion, Los
Angeles, in April 1983.

In Which We Serve 1942

At the age of nineteen, Richard Attenborough made his screen debut in this film whilst still a student at the Royal Academy of Dramatic Art. The story was based on part of Lord Louis Mountbatten's service in the Royal Navy during the Second World War. Later, Lord Louis was to figure prominently in Attenborough's endeavours to set up a film on the life of Mahatma Gandhi. *In Which We Serve* also marked the first of many occasions on which Attenborough was to appear on screen with John Mills.

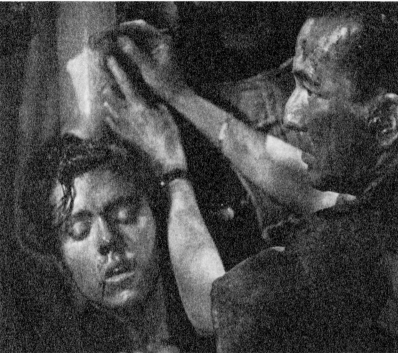

Apart from playing the lead, Noël Coward produced the film, co-directed and wrote both the screenplay and the score.

Adrift in the Carly float: (Left to right) RA, Michael Wilding, Geoffrey Hibbert, Bernard Miles, Derek Elphinstone, John Mills and John Boxer. Clinging on: Robert Sansom, Noël Coward, Caven Watson.

'Noël Coward's first British picture In Which We Serve is, in effect, a documentary with a human touch, and may be reckoned one of the best to come from a British studio.'
News Chronicle

'There should be high praise, too for a host of first-rate minor performances among the ship's company, particularly Mr Richard Attenborough.'
Time and Tide

Schweik's New Adventures 1943

Written as a sequel to the famous First World War series of
sketches by Jaroslav Kasek dealing with *The Good Soldier
Schweik* who was forced to fight in the Austro-Hungarian
Army, *Schweik's New Adventures* was based on a book
misleadingly entitled *How To Speak German Correctly*
published in occupied Prague during the Second World War.
The first few pages did deal with the subject described on the
cover but the main body of the book concerned Schweik's
encounters with the Gestapo. A copy was smuggled to England
and filmed by Karel Lamek. Attenborough, who was then laying
the foundations of his stage career in such West End
productions as *Brighton Rock*, played one of the smaller parts.

The Hundred Pound Window 1944

With Frederick Leister, Anne Crawford, David Farrar and
Mary Clare.

'This enigmatic title alludes to the
totalisator. Here the underworld
of wartime gambling and black-
marketing is curiously blended
into a film of English suburban
life.' Daily Telegraph

Journey Together 1945

Aircraftman Second Class Richard Attenborough was seconded from wartime pilot training to the RAF Film Unit to play the lead. Apart from providing the opportunity to work with two of Hollywood's legends, Edward G. Robinson and Bessie Love, it formed the basis of an enduring relationship with John Boulting who, together with his twin brother Roy, subsequently put Attenborough under contract. Following a press screening, the film correspondent of the *Daily Dispatch* wrote, 'Britain's first post-war film star was "born" yesterday. Richard Attenborough, who scuttled his acting career to join the RAF, made an instant hit in *Journey Together*.'

A scene with one of his great heroes, Edward G. Robinson, who played the Canadian flying instructor.

Bessie Love played Edward G. Robinson's wife and Jack Watling the other trainee pilot.

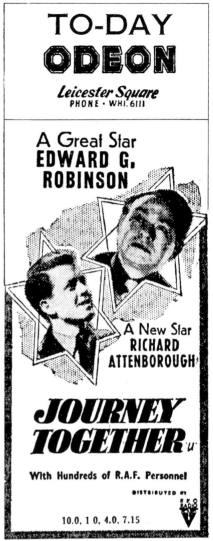

ABOVE
'The performance by that
starry-eyed youngster, Richard
Attenborough, gripped me so hard
that I found my hands stiff from
clutching the arm of my seat after
the solo flight that "scrubbed" him
as a pilot.'
Daily Mail

BELOW
This scene with Attenborough's
real-life fiancée, Sheila Sim,
finished on the cutting room floor.
They married in January 1945
whilst he was still in the Air Force.

A Matter of Life and Death 1946

'The Powell-Pressburger piece shows its creators not merely handling their material with easy authority, but enjoying the difficulties of the subject; using colour and monochrome . . . with a craftsman's pleasure in his medium.'
Dilys Powell, *Sunday Times*

With Kathleen Byron in the avant-garde post-war film that was to become a classic.

With Patrick Waddington, Ralph Richardson and John Laurie.
'How "boffins" (Services language for back-room scientists) invented that top-secret weapon of war, Radar, is the theme of School for Secrets, *another notable addition to British film achievement.'*
Sunday Pictorial

School for Secrets 1946

The Man Within 1947

Released in the United States under the title *The Smugglers*, this was a period piece in which Attenborough played his first—and last—romantic lead. His performance prompted this prediction from the *Los Angeles Times*: 'So little known was the young actor playing the youth that he received almost no billing, yet it is safe to say that he will become a star. His name is Richard Attenborough.' In Britain, where he was already a star, the *Daily Mirror* review read: 'Highlights of this Technicolor version of Graham Greene's colourful drama of smuggling in Sussex in olden times are the fine work of Richard Attenborough and Joan Greenwood. Richard is most convincing as a treacherous coward who reveals his manhood at the very last minute . . . An entertaining and, at times, distinctly gripping example of the psychological drama.'

With Joan Greenwood, a smuggler's daughter.

Suborned by Jean Kent, the mistress of a Crown barrister.

Flogged by Michael Redgrave.

Dancing with Crime 1947

Felix Barker wrote in the *Evening News*: 'Every now and again we are made suddenly aware that—politics and economics apart—we are living in a changed and divided England. A new set of people has come into being; with them have come different values and moral codes. *Dancing with Crime* is all snarls and shadows. You can almost smell the cheap scent of the dance floor and taste the black-market gin served at the chromium bar.'

'This view of English urban society is enlivened by some smart foot-and-fist-work by Richard Attenborough as a taxi-driver ready to go anywhere and take any fare, even a dead one.'
Sunday Times

BELOW
With his wife, Sheila Sim, and, on the right, an actor who was to become famous as Bill Owen. In this film, however, he appeared under his own name as Bill Rowbotham.

OPPOSITE ABOVE
Barry K. Barnes as the villain of the piece.

OPPOSITE BELOW
With Diana Dors, making what was probably her screen debut. Certainly Dancing with Crime *was Dirk Bogarde's first ever film but, sadly, no photograph survives to record the event.*

Brighton Rock 1948

Playing Pinkie, the villain of Graham Greene's story of gang warfare, provided Attenborough with the first really testing and complex role of his screen career. He had already created the character on the West End stage between completing his studies at RADA and volunteering for the RAF. The film version, co-scripted by Greene and Terence Rattigan and mostly shot on location in Brighton itself, marked the start of Attenborough's post-war collaboration with the Boulting brothers and received, with very few exceptions, tremendous acclaim.

OPPOSITE
Margaret Lane wrote in the
Evening Standard: *'Richard*
Attenborough's performance as
Pinkie Brown, the boy gangster, is
so good that one loses all sense of
its being a performance. He is
Pinkie the neurotic delinquent,
who still possesses the shreds of his
Catholic faith and a flicker of
childish charm.' *Leonard Mosley,*
however, stated of Attenborough's
casting in the Daily Express: *'The*
result, in my opinion, is that the
film version of Pinkie is about as
close to the real thing as Donald
Duck is to Greta Garbo.'

RIGHT
With Carol Marsh

BELOW
Slashed during a razor fight.

With Harcourt Williams who was one of RA's tutors at RADA and who, with Hermione Baddeley and William Hartnell, was in the original stage production.

With George Carney and Hermione Baddeley, playing Ida, the part she created on stage.

London Belongs To Me 1948

Though not intended solely to influence public opinion as was *10 Rillington Place* made two decades later, this film, adapted from Norman Collins's best-selling novel, was, in its own way, also a plea for the abolition of capital punishment. John Prebble wrote in the *Sunday Express*: 'Mr Attenborough is the one reason why you should see *London Belongs To Me*. As Percy Boon, the simple garage-hand turned to crime by calf-love, he gives so competent and moving a performance that you feel like joining the ridiculous rain-drenched procession that marches in protest against his conviction for murder.'

With Alistair Sim
Punch *1948.*

The Guinea Pig 1947

The second film to be made under Attenborough's post-war contract with the Boulting brothers. Although they had yet to develop the flair for satirical comedy that was to become their trademark, this film, in common with *Brighton Rock*, examined a live contemporary issue. 'It is a story,' wrote the *Manchester Guardian*'s London film critic 'of the son of a suburban tobacconist who is sent to one of Britain's prouder public schools; there he suffers, but "sticks it" and survives to be a credit to both his good, rough parents and to his good, much rougher school. Richard Attenborough is a young actor who seems to specialise in seeming younger still. All this film really depends on him. He bears it without falter.'

As a schoolboy opposite his wife, Sheila Sim, playing the part of his housemistress.

At home with Bernard Miles and
Joan Hickson.

'Richard Attenborough's portrayal
of the boy is so exceptionally real
that his use of a four-letter word
—the first time I have heard it
on the screen—was the only word
that could have been used in the
circumstances.' Evening Standard
(The word critic Milton Shulman
could not use in his review was
'arse'.)

Six of the best from Cecil
Trouncer.

The Lost People 1949

C. A. Lejeune wrote in the Observer: 'There must be a love story, so there is a love story, entailing the appearance of Richard Attenborough as a sort of village idiot; and Mai Zetterling as a cross between Dick Whittington and Bubbles—a shocking waste of two good players.'

Boys in Brown 1950

'The convincing story revolves around a Borstal institution and its inmates—boys who have been sent there for all kinds of crimes, ranging from larceny to murder.

'Richard Attenborough as one of the boys who joins in an escape plot, gives a wonderful performance, just as convincing as his *Guinea Pig*. Other borstal boys are cleverly played by Jimmy Hanley, Alfie Bass, Graham Payn and Dirk Bogarde.' *Daily Express*

With John Blythe, Dirk Bogarde and Michael Medwin in Boys in Brown.

Morning Departure 1950

This production had the unfortunate distinction of closely echoing an actual tragedy—the loss of the submarine HMS *Truculent*—which occurred whilst it was in post production tests. Despite some urging that the film be shelved indefinitely, after consultation with the Admiralty and the bereaved who lived mostly in the Medway towns, it opened on schedule to extremely laudatory reviews. Typical of the reaction is this opening paragraph by Campbell Dixon in the *Daily Telegraph*: 'While we can make films like *Morning Departure* the British screen has a future. Here are fighting men seen as they are, without false heroics or sickly sentiment. I don't know when I have been more moved.'

With James Hayter, John Mills and Nigel Patrick.

With James Hayter, Michael Brennan, Nigel Patrick, Victor Maddern, Andrew Crawford, George Cole and John Mills.

Hell is Sold Out 1951

Never screened in the West End of London, this film did well in the provinces. The *Manchester Evening News* critic wrote: 'It gives Richard Attenborough a chance to show what a good natural light comedian he is. Attenborough has been hankering after this for a long time.' Roger Lennox, writing in the *Bristol Evening World*, was, however, less flattering; '*Hell is Sold Out* tries its best to make entertainment out of the story of a pretty young writer who pretends she is a widow of a famous one—until he turns up. Mai Zetterling, Herbert Lom and Richard Attenborough are all very English in a photoplay which needs to be very French.'

With Mai Zetterling—again.

The Magic Box 1951

With Glynis Johns.

To celebrate the Festival of Britain, everyone who was anyone in the film industry pooled their acting talents to appear in The Magic Box. *It was a tribute to William Friese-Greene, a persistent inventor and the first man to produce and patent a commercially practicable motion-picture camera. Robert Donat played the lead and the glittering cast comprised sixty star names.*

50

Gift Horse 1952

Regarded by many as 'the mixture as before'. This view was encapsulated by Fred Majdalany who wrote in the *Daily Mail*: 'How many talking pictures are there to be extracted from a Fighting Service noted for its silence? I offer this as a thought for the week. The pattern of films about the Royal Navy— including *Gift Horse*, the latest—arouses suspicions in me that there are two: the one with a bit of a story and the one without. On the bridge there must be Trevor Howard (or John Mills) being grim and disciplinary; on the lower deck, Richard Attenborough being a nuisance.' Dilys Powell writing in the *Sunday Times* did, however, enjoy the film more than her colleagues and was of the opinion that this was Attenborough's best performance for years.

'Able performers like Richard Attenborough and Bernard Lee have been heaved overboard in a sea of roaring clichés.'
Milton Shulman, Evening Standard

Father's Doing Fine 1953

With Heather Thatcher and Noel Purcell in the screen adaptation of a successful drawing-room comedy.
'Mr Richard Attenborough rushes about a great deal, swallowing whisky and soda almost all the time, while waiting to become a father.'
Sussex Daily News

Eight O'Clock Walk 1954

'The story of a likeable young taxi-driver who is arrested on strong circumstantial evidence for the murder of a little girl. After the necessary preliminaries which show how an innocent man may find himself in this terrible predicament the piece settles down into a fairly absorbing Old Bailey trial drama and a consoling demonstration of the clear-sightedness of Justice.'
Financial Times

With Derek Farr and Cathy O'Donnell.

The Ship that Died of Shame 1955

From the prestigious Ealing Studios, this was Attenborough's first film with the producer-director team of Michael Relph and Basil Dearden. 'He is at his best,' wrote Dilys Powell of this performance in the *Sunday Times*.

'The Ship that Died of Shame *is a story by Mr Nicholas Monsarrat to whom the sea could appear to have been crueller than usual. It is all about a gallant little gunboat of the war whose naughty crew, led by Mr Richard Attenborough (with newcomer George Baker left)* force *it into a shameful post-war smuggling venture. Whereupon its poor little engines get so upset that they seize up and stutter to a stop.'*
Financial Times

Private's Progress 1956

The first of the anti-establishment satirical comedies that would become the hallmark of the Boulting brothers. This film also launched Ian Carmichael's film career with a great personal success. In the words of the *News of the World*, Attenborough portrayed 'the well-equipped barrack-room lawyer who can wangle anything from a railway warrant to a buckshee NAAFI feed'. Audiences and critics who, for years, had been accustomed to war films which invariably carried an expression of the producers' profound indebtedness to one or another of the Services were delighted by the Boultings' foreword gratefully acknowledging the official co-operation of absolutely nobody. The War Office had declined to be associated with the film 'because it was unlikely to assist recruiting'.

With Ian Carmichael.

'*There have been funny films before now about the British Army but never one quite like* Private's Progress. *This delightfully irreverent film "dedicated", as it says, "to those who get away with it", is about the Army scrounger, his hopes, his fears and elaborately evasive manner of life.*'
Manchester Guardian

With John Warren and Thorley Walters.

The Baby and the Battleship 1956

This marked the continuance of Attenborough's screen partnership with John Mills and the start of a close and enduring relationship with Bryan Forbes who both played in the film and co-wrote the script. Milton Shulman's *Sunday Express* review described Mills and Attenborough as being in so many navy films 'they will soon be walking with a list'. Shulman's notice was headlined 'Baby Takes All' and ended 'Every adult member of the cast should sympathise with W. C. Fields, who was asked after he made a film with Baby LeRoy, how he liked children. "Fried," was the reply.'

On location in Naples flanked by Michael Howard, John Mills, Bryan Forbes and some full-time serving members of the Royal Navy.

The Scamp 1957

With Dorothy Alison and Australian child star Colin Petersen in The Scamp. Of the character played by Attenborough The Times's reviewer wrote, 'The hero, clearly recognisable as such by his saintly forbearance, is a preparatory schoolmaster, equally recognisable as such by the large leather patch on each elbow of his jacket.'

Brothers in Law 1957

'The Boulting brothers have done it again. With Brothers in Law they establish themselves as the most original and successful vendors of British screen comedy in the business.'
Philip Oakes, Evening Standard

'Based on the book by Henry Cecil; hilarious brother-piece to Private's Progress *with the law as the object of satire this time. Witty and elegantly funny performances by Ian Carmichael, Richard Attenborough, Terry Thomas, Eric Barker, Irene Handl. For once I found a British film too short.'*
Dilys Powell, Sunday Times

With Ian Carmichael, Terry Thomas, Miles Malleson, and Eric Barker.

Dunkirk 1958

'Sir Michael Balcon began *Dunkirk*—his new film epic—long before television was the menace to the cinema that it is now. It cost him £500,000, and it needs an exceptional film to recoup that kind of money today. Because *Dunkirk* is exceptional I believe Sir Michael will get his money back.'
Ronald Maxwell, *Sunday Dispatch*.

'*Richard Attenborough, with a toothbrush moustache and rimless spectacles, lives the easy life in a reserved occupation outside London. He has a wife and a baby at home, all the petrol coupons he needs, and a safe job. Why should he worry? But when Dunkirk comes he too finds himself at the wheel of a small boat off the beaches.*'
Daily Express

'*Illuminated by stoic courage and now and then by sardonic humour—*Dunkirk *remains a severe film and some may complain that a sense of triumph is lacking, but it is present in the audience, for one comes out reflecting on the sacrifices of war and thinking gratefully: I have lived to look back on this terrible, this heroic moment in history. And that is itself a kind of triumph.*'
Dilys Powell, Sunday Times

RA and Patricia Plunkett contemplating, with horror a gas mask issued for their baby.

The Man Upstairs 1958

'The Association of Cine-Technicians,' wrote Paul Dehn in the *News Chronicle*, 'is a trade union which, some years ago, started its own production unit with a view to getting good, low-budgeted feature films made by its momentarily unemployed members. *The Man Upstairs* is the unit's twenty-first picture and one worth shouting about . . . Were I forced to grade individual contributions, I should single out Mr Attenborough's monumentally terrifying simulation of guilt spilling over into mania.'

The final scene with Kenneth Griffith, Edward Judd, Bernard Lee, Dorothy Alison, Donald Houston and Virginia Maskell.

Sea of Sand 1958

The Libyan desert featured prominently in this production.
When shooting was held up by the *gibli*—local name for a hot
sandstorm—the actors huddled together under groundsheets
until it passed, bemoaning the state of the British film industry
and describing what each would do to remedy it. Michael Craig
outlined an idea for a film he had hatched with his agent
brother, Richard Gregson; one that was unlike anything
currently in production. This was the basis, two years later, for
The Angry Silence, which marked Attenborough's first venture
into independent production.

*With Vincent Ball and Michael
Craig.*

'A desert winner . . . earns a row
of medals for director Guy Green
and a cast that performs with the
faultless brilliance of a hand-picked
élite.'
Evening Standard

Danger Within 1959

This film was co-scripted by Frank Harvey and Bryan Forbes.
Teasingly, the latter gave Attenborough's character a couple of
true-to-life attributes—an insatiable appetite for chocolate and
the name 'Bunter' which the habit had inspired. This resulted in
the following notice from Nancy Spain in the *Daily Express*:
'Richard Attenborough is the hero: a nice fattish little chap with
glasses. He is a member of an Escape Squad in a prison camp in
North Italy.'

*With Richard Todd, Vincent Ball,
William Franklyn, and Bernard
Lee.*

I'm All Right Jack 1959

The third and undoubtedly the most successful of the Boultings' satires and the last film in which Attenborough played for them. Harold Conway's review in the *Daily Sketch* is typical of the rapturous reception with which this production was greeted: 'Bang up to date, with cheerful audacity, Britain's irrepressible film team—John and Roy Boulting—have hurled their biggest-ever spanner into the works. They have now done what no previous movie-maker has dared attempt: to take the micky—brilliantly, uproariously—out of the trade union movement.'

'*Peter Sellers (with Hitlerite moustache) is the chief shop steward . . . using long words he can't pronounce, talking about Press Conferences, strutting around with the self-conscious air of a budding prime minister. It is the best, most devastating character study Sellers has yet given; his genius has been disciplined for the first time, and the goon becomes a most impressive actor.*'
Daily Sketch

With Margaret Rutherford, Dennis Price and Ian Carmichael.

Jetstorm 1959

With Mai Zetterling and Virginia Maskell.

'Jetstorm gets into the air on an Atlantic crossing a planeful of assorted passengers, then proceeds to threaten them with sudden death, a maniac (Richard Attenborough) having hidden a bomb on board . . . A large number of leading actors are involved in this fracas which they enter into bravely. Bravest man, though, was the script-writer who gave one of the passengers the remark, 'This is a nightmare; we should have gone by boat.' Sympathy and loud laughter.'
Daily Telegraph.

'In a story of this kind the convincing behaviour of the characters must be a major factor. In his soft, spongy silence, Mr Attenborough himself is formidable.'
Observer.

SOS Pacific 1959

'Eddie Constantine as the rugged hero and Richard Attenborough as a nervy spiv steal the show. Addicts of the rough-necked school will revel in this hokum.'
News of the World.

The Angry Silence 1960

An important milestone for Attenborough marking the point in his career where he became a film maker as well as a screen actor. The broader significance of this production was that, unusually for the time, it dealt uncompromisingly with a subject of contemporary social significance. Attenborough had become increasingly disillusioned with the parts he was being offered. He decided, together with Bryan Forbes, to embark on independent production under the aegis of their own company, Beaver Films. They approached the Boulting brothers, as board members of British Lion, for finance and were offered just over 70% of the figure needed. After trying, abortively, to trim their budget down to the £100,000 British Lion was prepared to invest, they solved the problem by persuading a number of key people involved in the production to join them in accepting a percentage of eventual profits in lieu of salary. Wth Attenborough playing the lead and, for the very first time, co-producing, the film was made for only £97,000. The result was a huge critical success and, in the long run, also a commercial one with all the participants earning more in deferred payments than they had originally relinquished.

'This is a brilliant and haunting picture dealing with the problems of the factory and the bench — which is the place where most of the British people work.

'British films sometimes make me despair. But now and then you get a beauty like The Angry Silence and you realise that deep in the heart of this anxious, disturbed industry there are writers, directors and actors who both know and care.'
Cassandra, Daily Mirror.

With Pier Angeli.

'You will not recognise this brand of trade unionism since it does not exist in Britain. It was invented by the film-makers. It is a lying travesty of the way British working men and women behave.'
Nina Hibbin, Daily Worker.

'To call it a brave film would be misleading because it might imply that in Britain some sort of permit attended such frank speech; but frank, angry, skilful and convincing it certainly is.'
Guardian.

'Humbly and most sincerely I salute today the courage and, yes, the genius of Richard Attenborough. He has produced a topical, controversial, vitriolic masterpiece.'
Donald Gomery, Daily Express.

With Bernard Lee and Pier Angeli.

With Michael Craig.

'They're giving me the old "Angry Silence".'

63

The League of Gentlemen 1960

'I enjoyed every felonious moment of *The League of Gentlemen*,' wrote C. A. Lejeune in the *Observer*. 'It is a beautifully bloodless thriller which describes the planning and execution of a big bank robbery, by a group of slightly shady ex-officers briefed to regard the operation as a text-book military campaign.'

At the 1960 San Sebastian Film Festival all eight leading members of the film's cast received the Zulueta Best Actor Award.

Clockwise from RA: Nigel Patrick, Kieron Moore, Norman Bird, Terence Alexander, Director Basil Dearden, First Assistant Director, George Pollard, Camera Operator, Bob Thompson, Jack Hawkins, Continuity Girl, Penny Daniels, Director of Photography, Arthur Ibbetson, Bryan Forbes and Roger Livesey.

Whistle Down the Wind 1960

'The three children, having taken their gifts, run out of the barn to the top of the hilly field and dance, against the sky-line, their own ecstatic version of the ancient minor-mode Coventry Carol ('We Three Kings of Orient Are') . . . Such minutes as these, in this simple-hearted film, mean far more than whole hours in million-dollar biblical epics.'
Alan Dent, Sunday Telegraph.

Based on a book by Mary Hayley Bell, mother of leading player, Hayley Mills, this was also the film in which Alan Bates made his screen debut. It was produced by Attenborough and directed by Bryan Forbes for their company, Beaver Films, and received on both sides of the Atlantic such rave reviews as these:
'All merit, praise and affection for giving us one of the most enjoyable and heart-warming films we've ever seen.'
Bosley Crowther, *New York Times*
'This modest British masterpiece miraculously manages to be unmawkish about a child's belief in Christ's second coming.'
Paul Dehn, *Daily Herald*.

Only Two Can Play 1962

With Virginia Maskell.

'Richard Attenborough gives a wicked little parody of a Welsh poet.'
Nina Hibben, Daily Worker.

Alan Dent described this film in the Sunday Telegraph *as 'a wry and sly examination into the dream-world of an oversexed Welsh librarian,' (Sellers) and added, 'Richard Attenborough is brilliant as an awful little weed of a Welsh playwright.'*

With Peter Sellers and Mai Zetterling.

The L-Shaped Room 1962

Leslie Caron and Tom Bell played the leads in this film which was produced jointly by Attenborough and James Woolf. It was written for the screen and directed by Bryan Forbes. Peter Baker wrote in Films & Filming: 'The L-Shaped Room tries for a kind of honesty that we know to be inherent in the makers of The Angry Silence and Whistle Down The Wind. Forbes and Attenborough don't respond to the problem of living in the same way as Richardson, Reisz or Schlesinger. But there are times when I sense they feel more passionately about it.'

With Paul Harris and Dave Brubeck in this modern-dress version of Othello.

All Night Long 1962

The Dock Brief 1962

In this two-hander, adapted from John Mortimer's play, Richard Attenborough and Peter Sellers appeared together for the first time since the latter had leapt to film stardom with *I'm All Right Jack*. The *Daily Mirror* review was headlined: 'A Duel in the Dock—and Attenborough Outpoints Sellers.' Their critic went on, 'Richard Attenborough turns in a performance which puts even the brilliantly versatile Peter Sellers in the shade in *The Dock Brief*. With a moustache and a slightly built up nose to help, Attenborough emerges as a seedy, pathetic little character in a fascinating film mixture of fantasy, irony, comedy, drama and pathos.' The *Guardian*'s critic saw the film more as a meeting of equals, writing, 'Acting of superlative reality by the two men concerned. From Peter Sellers we have, long since, come to expect a great deal; so his fine performance with the wry comedy of its brittle optimism and frail pomposity is no great surprise. From Mr Attenborough, accomplished actor though he has long been, we had no reason to expect anything comparable; his acting—as the gentlest, most involuntary and least self-centred of murderers—is all the more noteworthy.'

Assuming the role of judge as, in his cell, the murderer helps his counsel envisage masterful arguments for the defence.

Peter Sellers played the unsuccessful barrister who gets the chance of a lifetime with a dock brief to defend Attenborough who is accused of murdering his nagging wife.

The acquitted and his counsel at the prison gate.

The Great Escape 1963

So far Attenborough's screen performances had only been seen in the USA on the 'art house' circuits reserved for imported productions. Now, for the first time with United Artists distributing, he starred in a film which was seen throughout America. The following review appeared in *Variety*: 'Since there are no marquee "naturals" in the cast, this picture will illustrate how superior story and production values can carry a project to great success without the aid of prohibitively expensive souped-up stellar names. It's still the picture that counts, not necessarily who's in it . . .

'British thespians weigh in with some of the finest performances in the picture. Richard Attenborough is especially convincing in a stellar role, that of the man who devises the break.'

With Gordon Jackson and Donald Pleasance.

'*The Great Escape is a gorgeous movie adventure. By a gorgeous movie I mean something with blood in its veins, humor in its heart, adventure in its action, skill in its mind. This crackles from the word go . . . Attenborough, always within his characters, never has been better than the imaginative, silently strong "Mr. X".*'
Richard L. Coe, Washington Post.

With Charles Bronson, Gordon Jackson, James Coburn, Steve McQueen, Donald Pleasance, James Garner and John Leyton.

With Steve McQueen.

'The story is based on Paul Brickhill's true account of a meticulously planned mass break-out
from a supposedly impregnable
camp housing as expert a team of
'cracksmen' as the Germans could
have assembled.
  'Organised, in one of Richard
Attenborough's best performances,
by a squadron leader seasoned in
the arts of escape, they plot the
perfect dig for freedom.'
Cecil Wilson, Daily Mail.

*With Nigel Stock, William Russell
and James Coburn.*

Seance on a Wet Afternoon 1964

This production was the last on which Attenborough and Bryan Forbes worked in partnership. The former, who won Best Actor awards from the San Sebastian Film Festival and the British Academy for his performance, was by now deeply embroiled in trying to mount *Gandhi*. Kim Stanley, the celebrated American actress who played opposite Attenborough, received an Oscar nomination for her portrayal of a neurotic medium.

'When acting awards are given this year, a few should go to Kim Stanley for *Seance on a Wet Afternoon*. And two others for the film itself and Richard Attenborough who partners her in this powerful psychological thriller which is so much more than just another suspense movie. The film is not only excellent entertainment. It is also a superlative example of how the screen can be better than the stage as a showcase for flawless acting.' Frances Herridge, *New York Post*.

'Seance on a Wet Afternoon *is the perfect psychological suspense thriller and a flawless film to boot.'* Judith Crist, New York Herald Tribune.

'In the file I keep in the back of my brain for memorable moments, this film has been slipped to be savoured and enjoyed for all time.' Leonard Mosley, Daily Express.

Stanley and Attenborough at the final seance with Patrick Magee and Gerald Sim.

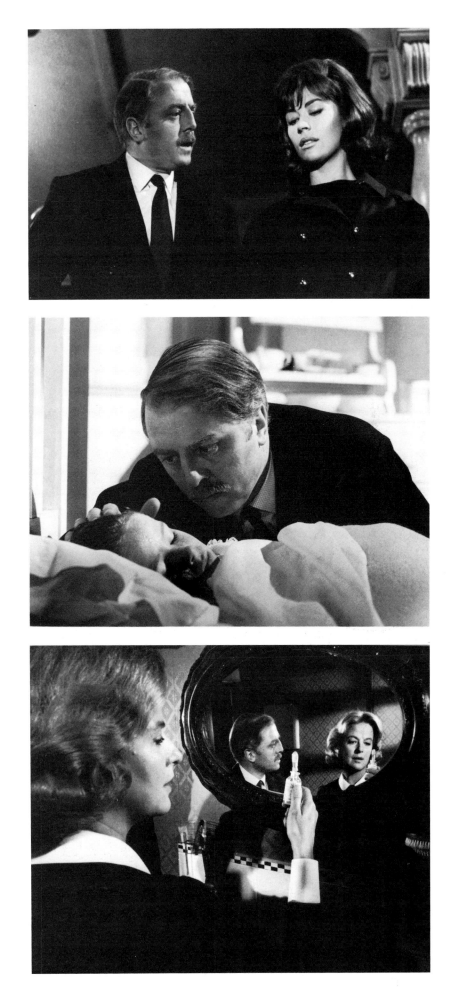

With Nanette Newman as the child's mother.

With Judith Donner as the kid-napped child.

'As soloists Kim Stanley and Richard Attenborough are remark-able; in concert their perform-ances merit a dozen or more Oscars at the current rate.'
Sunday Telegraph.

'Mr Attenborough . . . improves and improves; in fact he has been a winner ever since he stopped playing the series of panicky naval ratings and the like which began with In Which We Serve.'
Dilys Powell, Sunday Times.

The Third Secret 1964

'Among so many films that are supercolossal (by definition) or simply (by aesthetic miscalculation) inflated, one sometimes yearns for the modest, middling picture that, since so few directors will admit to middling intentions let alone talents, so seldom turns up.

'*The Third Secret* is just such a film, a rarity therefore and something of a treat . . . Richard Attenborough, Jack Hawkins and Diane Cilento are all excellently uneasy, ambiguously directed to arouse sympathy and suspicion'. *The Spectator*.

As a painter turned art-dealer with Patience Collier.

With Stephen Boyd.

Guns At Batasi 1964

This performance is believed by many critics to be Attenborough's finest, although personally he does not rate it as highly as *Seance on a Wet Afternoon*. Both portrayals resulted in his winning the British Academy's Best Actor award. Typical of rave reviews, on both sides of the Atlantic, is Ian Crawford's notice in the *Sunday Express*: 'The film belongs to Richard Attenborough who gives a magnificent performance as Lauderdale, full of stuffy fire, regimental bombast, and a kind of glory behind the closed mind and the Service-burnished exterior. He makes the Regimental Sergeant-Major a man who touches your heart even when every liberal instinct urges you to hate everything he represents. This is acting with every tautened muscle of the body, every meticulously studied nuance of the brassy voice, every brain cell intent on creating a man from the inside out.'

'*What matters most in* Guns at Batasi *is the performance of Richard Attenborough. After 21 years of banking his professional fire he here lets it blaze into a life-size portrait of a professional soldier; an RSM, no less, coping with mutiny in an emergent African state, with nothing but his wits and Queen's Regulations to sustain him.*'
Philip Oakes, Sunday Telegraph.

With Flora Robson.

With Jack Hawkins.

With John Leyton and Mia Farrow.

The Flight of the Phoenix 1966

With Dan Durea, Ronald Fraser, Ernest Borgnine, Alex Montoya, Ian Bannen, Peter Finch, Christian Marquand, George Kennedy and James Stewart.

This was the first of three successive Hollywood films in which Attenborough was to play. In spite of its star cast and prestigious director/producer, Robert Aldrich, the production did not fare well at the hands of critics when it was first shown, although in latter years it has gained tremendously in stature.

With James Stewart and Hardy Kruger.

'The Flight of the Phoenix *is lucky to have such a thumping cast of stars, headed by the unflappable Jimmy Stewart and the unsinkable Dickie Attenborough. Not to mention all those talented people who support them. And a monkey! They make one of those crummy stories, about a plane crashing in the desert and what happens to the survivors, look like new.'*
Ernest Betts, The People.

HARDY KRUGER as Heinrich Dorfmann, JAMES STEWART as Frank Towns and RICHARD ATTENBOROUGH as Lew Moran in *The Flight of the Phoenix*

The Sand Pebbles 1967

'McQueen's Film, but Watch Attenborough Live his Part,' was the headline to Alexander Walker's review in the Evening Standard. It went on: 'Attenborough, sporting a moustache you could call a 'half Fu-Manchu', not only puts on an impeccably American accent but please note how brilliantly he even adapts the posture of his body, the tempo of his movements to US specifications. The film belongs to him and Steve McQueen—one plays the part, the other is the part. Both are, in their separate ways, on top form.'

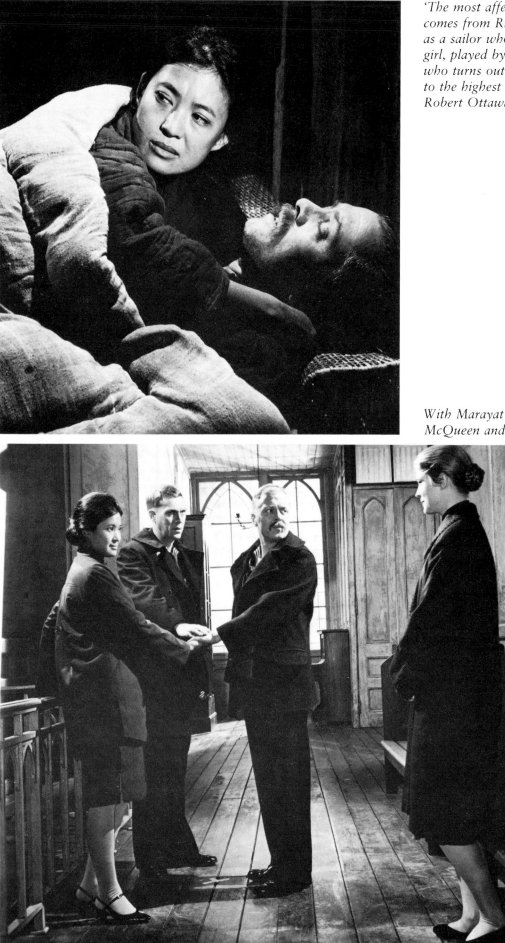

'The most affecting performance comes from Richard Attenborough as a sailor who falls for a Chinese girl, played by Marayat Andriane, who turns out pure but is available to the highest bidder in a brothel.' Robert Ottaway, Daily Sketch.

With Marayat Andriane, Steve McQueen and Candice Bergen.

Dr Dolittle 1967

Attenborough's long stay in Hollywood which started with *The Flight of the Phoenix* and led to playing an American sailor in *The Sand Pebbles* (for which he won his first Best Supporting Actor Golden Globe from the film colony's Foreign Press Association at the 1966 ceremony), culminated in his most unlikely casting in *Dr Dolittle*. This small but arduous part demanded not only a song but also a minutely choreographed dance which, although he approached both with trepidation, resulted in another Golden Globe, presented in 1967.

The Variety critic wrote of his performance; 'Outstanding is Richard Attenborough as Albert Blossom, the circus owner. He comes on so strong in his one song-and-dance bit (considering he's thought of only as a dramatic actor) that it's nearly a perfect example of why important cameo roles should be turned over to important talents.'

'Richard Attenborough has a marvellous demonic spot as Blossom, a circus owner, cutting capers and hitting notes as if his heart were on loan to the film's financiers.'
John Coleman, New Statesman.

'Richard Attenborough is a complete delight and just about walks off with the show.'
Judith Crist.

'It is Richard Attenborough's single song of delighted amazement accompanied by an appropriate dance at getting for his circus such a rare beast as the Pushmi-Pullyu—a twin-headed lama—that really raises the roof.'
Patrick Gibbs, Daily Telegraph.

With Muriel Landers and Rex Harrison.

Only When I Larf 1968

Adapted from Len Deighton's novel, directed by Basil Dearden and featuring Attenborough, David Hemmings and Alexandra Stewart as a team of confidence tricksters who employ numerous forms of disguise.

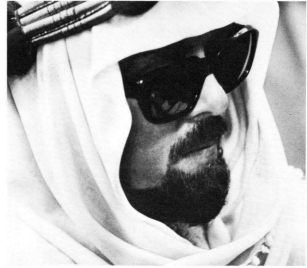

'Richard Attenborough enjoying one of the best roles of his career as the leader of a trio of swindlers, maintains that he is doing our capitalist society a favour by ruining the greedy and the gullible. This gives him the chance to play several roles and he plays them all magnificently.' Ian Christie, Daily Express.

'Only afterwards does one realise just how superb is Attenborough's performance which is a sign of just how superb it is. The external detail is, as always, impeccable; he's quite unlike many actors who, outwardly so convincing, can't seem to muster the inner man. There is a moment, no more than a flicker, when he realises that the lad he's brought on and privately despises is taking over—and more, has a right to take over. I shan't forget it in a hurry.' Margaret Hinxman, Sunday Telegraph.

The Bliss of Mrs Blossom 1968

Frances Herridge of the *New York Post* wrote: 'The joke is told in a manner that combines French bedroom farce with mod British tomfoolery. If offers the considerable talents of Richard Attenborough as a busy bra manufacturer ('Orpheus of the Undie World'), Shirley MacLaine as the delectable wife who had spent too many hours alone, and James Booth who came to repair the sewing machine and stayed on in the attic to fill her daytime hours.'

With Shirley MacLaine.

'The film has a potty and capricious charm that is quite unexpected. Mr Blossom, improbably but perfectly played by Richard Attenborough, manufactures brassieres. He is clearly a dedicated man, with his mind purely on the business curves of his profession.' Madeleine Harmsworth, Sunday Mirror.

With Frank Thornton and Patricia Routledge.

Oh! What A Lovely War 1969

Seldom, if ever, can a directorial debut have been acclaimed in such unanimously glowing terms. This production also won a total of sixteen international awards of which the most prized was the British Academy's United Nations accolade. David Robinson wrote in the *Financial Times*: 'To film *Oh! What a Lovely War* looked like an unwise, if not impossible undertaking. Its particular kind of stylisation—it lay somewhere between concert party, music hall, political revue and anthology—belonged so completely to the theatre. And even while watching the film and seeing its successes, you cannot avoid a nervous feeling that Richard Attenborough will still not bring it off—right to the end, in fact, when you realise with admiration that he has brought it off; and to a large degree, triumphantly.'

RIGHT
The Smith family played by Angela Thorne, John Rae, Mary Wimbush, Corin Redgrave, Maurice Roeves, Kim Smith, Colin Farrel, Malcolm McFee, Paul Shelley, Wendy Allnutt and Kathleen Wileman.

BELOW
Ralph Richardson as Sir Edward Grey, Kenneth More as Kaiser Wilhelm II, Ian Holm as Premier Poincaré of France and John Gabriel as Lenin. Seated is Frank Forsyth as President Woodrow Wilson.

*Dirk Bogarde as Stephen and
Susannah York as Eleanor.*

'A fantasy, beautiful, dreadful,
heartbreaking. I found it impossible to restrain my tears.'
Dilys Powell, Sunday Times.

In the trenches.

'Here, the word "masterpiece" is
appropriate and I am glad to use
it.'
Derek Malcolm, The Guardian.

*Jack Hawkins as the Emperor
Franz Joseph with John Gielgud as
Count Berchtold.*

'A film that will be cherished as
long as the cinema has a history.'
Margaret Hinxman, Sunday Telegraph.

Maggie Smith as a music hall star.

'*Richard Attenborough's debut as a film director is an occasion that warrants such often overused, but not in this case, showbiz verbal coinage as "fabulous", "sensational", "stupendous" etc. His work also happens to be dedicated, exhilarating, shrewd, mocking, funny, emotional, witty, poignant and technically brilliant.*'
Variety.

Laurence Olivier as Field Marshal Sir John French dancing with Isabel Dean.

'*It is not merely the best film of 1969 but an oustanding film about war that is worth the tens of thousands of words perpetually mouthed about war. A movie derived from a stage musical, it so transcends its source that it stands on its own as a creative motion picture . . . Attenborough has brought to it the impeccable taste and professionalism that have been the hallmarks of his acting career.*'
Judith Crist, New York Magazine.

Vanessa Redgrave as Sylvia Pank-hurst.

'The whole cinema is bursting with a dead, dead generation and every heart in the audience is bursting with tears. The young and the old contemptibles are equally moved. We sit there—our own execution-ers.

'This brilliant film by Atten-borough should be made compul-sory viewing for all, particularly those whose ambitions allow their fingers near the button.

'Oh! What A Lovely War *is worth a million demonstrations. It kicks the hell out of jingoism and makes Attenborough one of the great directors of cinema art.'*
Fergus Cashin, Daily Sketch.

John Mills as Field Marshal Haig.

The Magic Christian 1969

Alexander Walker wrote in the
Evening Standard: *'Peter Sellers*
plays Sir Guy Grand and Ringo
Starr his adopted dropout son. . .
Sir Guy is as fantasticated as the
people he bribes and corrupts. He
slips Richard Attenborough a
sweetener to talk his Oxford Boat-
race crew into cutting the Cam-
bridge rudder and cause havoc in
the tideway. The sacred cow of
sportsmanship is the target. But it's
so badly set up you don't notice it
being hit.'

The Last Grenade 1970

'Here told by his wife that she has
fallen in love and wants a divorce,
Richard Attenborough as a bone-
headed British general is called
on, poor chap, to deliver the vener-
able line: "Might I ask the name of
this -er?" The name, should you
wish to read further, is Grigsby
(Stanley Baker).'
Dilys Powell, Sunday Times.

With Honor Blackman.

David Copperfield 1970

'The twin triumphs of the film, in their short scene together, are
Laurence Olivier as the vicious headmaster Mr Creakle and
Richard Attenborough as Mr Tungay his peg-legged sidekick.
Olivier's classroom threats are pitched in a barely audible voice—
while Attenborough repeats them in a parade-ground echo of
his master's whisper. A perfect Dickensian double act.'
Alexander Walker, *Evening Standard*.

Loot 1970

'Loot *is a sort of bedroom farce with a body. The corpse that makes way for the money is treated like a sack of coal to be unceremoniously dumped at will throughout this whole macabre merry-go-round. Hywel Bennett, Roy Holder, Lee Remick and Milo O'Shea do their ghoulish best—but the real light in all this blackness is Richard Attenborough. As the posturing policeman on the trail of the loot, he turns in a bravura performance. It's worth a visit just to see him.'*
David Gillard, Daily Sketch.

With Milo O'Shea and
Lee Remick.

A Severed Head 1971

'The fundamental tension of the film derives from the fact that everyone—but most especially the psychiatrist, brilliantly played by that most versatile of actors, Richard Attenborough—is convinced that he is being perfectly intelligent and rational. All, in fact, are moved by unknowable forces, are at all times lying to themselves without even knowing it.

'Nobody's going to call *A Severed Head* a real old fashioned movie-movie. In fact there's no convenient catch phrase that accurately summarizes it. Maybe one should just call it indescribably delicious and let it go at that.' Richard Schickel, *Life Magazine*.   *With Lee Remick.*

10 Rillington Place 1971

Vincent Canby, *New York Times*: 'Early in the morning of 9 March 1950, after a good night's sleep, Timothy John Evans, a 25-year-old Welshman with the mind of a child, was executed for the murder of his infant daughter, Geraldine. It was also believed that Evans had murdered his wife, Beryl . . .

'Three years later, the Evanses' landlord, John Reginald Christie, a former policeman who had been the chief prosecution witness at the trial, was himself arrested and charged with the murder of his wife, Ethel, whose body had been discovered under the floorboards of 10 Rillington Place. Ethel wasn't the only one stashed away at that shabby address. Investigation revealed five more bodies hidden in kitchen cupboards and buried in the back yard, and before Christie was hanged on 15 July 1953, he confessed to all these murders, as well as Beryl's.

A later inquiry into the murders, and into the two trials, resulted in a posthumous pardon for Evans and the abolition of the death penalty.

'This is a real life case on which Richard Fleischer, the director and Clive Exton, the scenarist, have based *10 Rillington Place*, using Ludovic Kennedy's book of the same title as their source material.'

'Nothing is glamourised, nothing sensationalised. Richard Attenborough, faced with the difficult task of playing a man who was in every way except one the quintessence even of nothingness, does a superb job and is matched by John Hurt as Evans.'
John Russell Taylor, Financial Times.

'A model of restraint in the manner of its telling, 10 Rillington Place marks another high point in Richard Attenborough's career. Once again he gives one of his utterly complete performances, the kind in which the actor is totally absorbed into the character he is playing, in this instance a mediocre but cunning fiend, a man so gripped by insane passion that he is a figure of pity until . . .'
Kevin Thomas, Los Angeles Times.

Young Winston 1972

Richard Attenborough's second film as a director was *Young Winston* with a screenplay by producer Carl Foreman based on Churchill's own memoirs, *My Early Years*. The story traced formative events in the future stateman's life from childhood to the age of 26 when he made his first major speech in the House of Commons. Under a headline that read: 'An Even Greater Film Than Lawrence of Arabia', Felix Barker wrote in the *Evening News*: 'In a production so full of subtleties, I have only space to praise one aspect of Richard Attenborough's brilliant unobtrusive direction. The man who displayed so much virtuosity in *Oh! What A Lovely War* is here content to paint his canvas with modest delicacy and a perfect sense of period.'

Anne Bancroft and Robert Shaw as Lord and Lady Randolph Churchill.

'Director Richard Attenborough has recreated with great skill the final halcyon days of the British Empire—a time of rigid morality, ultra-conscientious self-discipline and unsurpassed elegance.' Richard Cuskelly, Los Angeles Herald Examiner.

The schoolboy Winston delivering the Oration at Harrow.

Anne Bancroft as Lady Randolph Churchill with Russell Lewis as Winston, aged seven.

'Controlling it all, the sober but sensitive directorial hand of Richard Attenborough . . . There is nothing here quite to match the imaginative and emotional lift of the best moments in Oh! What A Lovely War but nothing either to contradict our first opinion of Mr Attenborough's considerable talents as a director as well as an actor.'
John Russell Taylor, The Times.

Simon Ward as Young Winston with Robert Shaw.

Boers ambush an armoured train.

John Mills as General Sir Herbert Kitchener.

'Richard Attenborough's expert direction proves that Oh! What A Lovely War was no flash in the pan. He calls the film an intimate epic and so it is.'
Cecil Wilson, Daily Mail.

The newly elected MP for Oldham makes his maiden speech.

'Among the most precarious films to make are biographies of renowned contemporary figures. Director, Richard Attenborough has the taste and perspective to survive the pitfalls and create an engaging, absorbing and entertaining story about Winston Churchill's early years.'
William Wolf, Cue Magazine, New York.

Rosebud 1975

Brannigan 1975

John Wayne and Richard Attenborough in "Brannigan."

ABOVE
'There was a certain fascination, I found, in watching O'Toole adapt his lounge-lizardly ways to the role of an action man, while Richard Attenborough as a renegade British mercenary in charge of Arab terrorists is essential viewing. Beseeching Allah to let him know why he has been forsaken in the last reel, Attenborough is favoured with the reply of one of his captors, "Perhaps you embarrassed him." Much the same could and should be said of the film as a whole.'
The Observer.

LEFT
'The characters are well drawn by a strong cast. There's some effective photography of familiar London scenes and a superbly filmed car chase over Tower Bridge.
'But for me the high point was seeing Richard Attenborough sock Wayne on the jaw.'
David Wigg, Daily Express.

Conduct Unbecoming 1975

Adapted from a stage play by Barry England, this film was directed by Michael Anderson whose first encounter with Attenborough had been as first assistant director on In Which We Serve. The prestigious cast included Michael York, Trevor Howard, Stacy Keach, Christopher Plummer, Susannah York, James Faulkner, Michael Culver, James Donald and Helen Cherry.

And Then There Were None 1975

With Adolpho Celi, Gert Froebe, Stephane Audran, Oliver Reed, Herbert Lom, Charles Aznavour and Elke Sommer.

A Bridge Too Far 1977

Attenborough's third film as a director was a massive undertaking. Shot over six months in Holland, it documented and dramatised the nine days of Operation Market Garden, the bold single thrust with which the Allies aimed at terminating World War II by the winter of 1944. Alan Brien wrote of it in the *Sunday Times*: 'If you are going to see only one war film in the next five years, then Richard Attenborough's *A Bridge Too Far* may be epic enough. There linger, on the retina, image after image of the Arnhem operation—parachutes popping out of a squadron of planes, like eggs laid in the slipstream by pregnant, silver fish; a creeping barrage of scarlet star shells precisely over-running the stolid ranks of German anti-tank gunners, waiting in ambush; the glistening, sweat-pearled faces of paratroopers retreating at night through a twitching forest of livid leaves . . . The thin irony of *Oh! What A Lovely War* has curdled into the heavy satire of War is Hell.'

Liv Ullman as Kate Ter Horst with Laurence Olivier as Doctor Spaander.

Robert Redford as Major Cook.

Hardy Kruger as Major-General Ludwig.

Maximilian Schell as Lieutenant-General Bittrich.

Sean Connery as Major-General Urquhart.

Anthony Hopkins as Lieutenant-Colonel Frost.

James Caan (centre) in a scene
with Arthur Hill and Garrick
Hagon.

'This is a war film that lingers in
the mind and the retina.'
Milton Shulman, Vogue.

'This is Attenborough's triumph.
He deserves loud and resounding
cheers for his direction.'
Judith Crist, NBC News.

'Among the best recreated movie
combat footage I have ever seen.'
Philip French, The Times.

'A magnificent war film. The battle
scenes are superbly done, seldom
equalled, never bettered.'
Bernard McElwaine, Sunday Mirror.

"Attenborough deserves great credit for the intelligence and integrity
of this film with superb work by
production designer, Terry Marsh,
editor Anthony Gibbs and especially cinematographer, Geoffrey Unsworth."
Jack Kroll, Newsweek.

Elliott Gould, as Colonel Stout,
leading a charge.

'What Attenborough has brought
off seems not just admirable but
astonishing. A war film both
monumental in its scale and sur-
prising in its subtlety.'
Charles Champlin, Los Angeles
Times.

'In sequences that will leave you
shell-shocked, riven and aghast, the
film recreates the sheer hell of war,
with enormous power.'
Richard Barkley, Sunday Express.

ABOVE
At Arnhem—the bridge that was too far.

RIGHT
Gene Hackman as the Polish Major-General Sosabowski, Ryan O'Neal as the American Brigadier-General Gavin, Michael Caine as Lieutenant-Colonel J. O. E. Vandeleur, Edward Fox as Lieutenant-General Horrocks and Dirk Bogarde as Lieutenant-General Browning.

'A masterpiece. The greatest war film ever made.'
Chris Kenworthy, The Sun.

The Chess Players 1978

Satyajit Ray is one of the directors Attenborough most admires and when, after the completion of *A Bridge Too Far*, Ray asked him to play in *The Chess Players*, he leapt at the chance. His scenes were filmed during the hot season in Calcutta and, for most of them, he wore a thick, tightly fitting scarlet uniform. As there was no air conditioning and the temperature in the studios rarely fell below 140°F, ice packs were applied to Attenborough's head and neck until the moment the camera started to turn. Ray would only call a halt to the take when the actor was too visibly bathed in sweat to continue.

'Satyajit Ray's *The Chess Players* is a masterly, fascinating, intricate movie which equates the obsessive passion for playing chess of the two principal characters, a couple of Lucknow noblemen, with the British take-over of an Indian State from an effete but dignified ruler.

'The period, of course, is the mid nineteenth century, the time of the British Raj. As the British resident general, Richard Attenborough has never given a finer performance.' Margaret Hinxman, Daily Mail.

'A fine film, with a central all-sustaining performance by Attenborough that should win him a top acting award.' Felix Barker, *Evening News*.

With Tom Alter and Amjad Khan as the king.

Magic 1978

Of Attenborough's five films as a director only this has no basis in biography or history. It was filmed entirely in the United States. Nicholas Wapshott wrote in the *Scotsman*: 'Attenborough finally convinced the Americans of his competence with a star cast and a large budget with *A Bridge Too Far*. Here he has maintained the Hollywood class and revived some of the supernatural air of *Seance on a Wet Afternoon*. His stage experience gives him the knack of being able to manage actors while giving them the chance to show off their best.'

'Magic *is an eery but brilliantly effective psychological thriller that, to my taste, beats any film ever made by the alleged master of the genre, Alfred Hitchcock.'*
Richard Grenier, Cosmopolitan.

'What the film proves is that Attenborough is a darned good director of actors. As Corky, Anthony Hopkins gives a sweaty anxious performance I'd never believe he was able to manage. Ann-Margret is frankly magical— sorry!—as Corky's ageing sweetheart involved in a loveless marriage.'
Margaret Hinxman, Daily Mail.

'Polished grand guignol—Richard Attenborough captures the atmosphere so powerfully that one finds one's self shivering.'
Philip French, The Observer.

Anthony Hopkins with Fats, the dummy.

'Richard Attenborough's direction is impeccable. Certain British directors have a sense of economy about storytelling that's refreshing to behold. I can't recall the last American film I've seen in which such attention was paid to acting.' Bruce McCabe, Boston Globe.

'Richard Attenborough's tale of mystery and imagination is scripted by William Goldman from his best seller. "Magic is a misdirection," is the key-phrase of the movie and it is Attenborough's skill that, while expecting melodrama, what we in fact get is a moving study of human relationships.'
Tom Hutchinson, Sunday Telegraph.

BELOW
Burgess Meredith as the theatrical agent.

The Human Factor 1980

With John Gielgud.

'Attenborough's muddlesome Colonel Daintry wields a rosy cheek and a fine pair of mutton-chops as he blunders genteelly into (Nicol) Williamson's guilt, and Preminger wisely lets him steal as many scenes as he can. Attenborough looks as if he's discovering and relishing his role as he goes along.'
Nigel Andrews, Financial Times.

'Richard Attenborough, though oddly cast, transcends that with a splendid performance as the colonel assigned to track down the double agent, desperately ill at ease without the comforting cloak of his work.'
Derek Malcolm, Guardian.

BELOW
With Nicol Williamson, Robert Morley and Derek Jacobi.

Gandhi 1982

This production which Attenborough had endeavoured to mount for twenty years had its world première in New Delhi, followed, within the same week, by openings in London, Washington, Toronto, New York and Los Angeles. With very few exceptions, the reviews for the first film he had ever both produced and directed were in similar vein to David Hughes writing in the *Sunday Times*: 'I must tell you first that *Gandhi* is a masterpiece. Also its arrival on the screen is a masterly piece of timing. In range of content, nobility of purpose and generosity of spirit Sir Richard Attenborough's achievement coincides with a national longing for just the kind of heart's ease he dispenses. The film is inspired because it offers inspiration . . . Sir Richard is often heckled for his lack of individual style as a director. He can rest easy. Here with love, with truth, he serves Gandhi well by giving an immensely personal account of him, but on a political scale that travels far beyond the borders of India into the heart of our lives at home.'

Ben Kingsley as Mahatma Gandhi goes, at last, to parlay on equal terms with the representative of the King Emperor in New Delhi.

'*The ultimate triumph for Attenborough and Kingsley that can be felt by all, is in making us realise the extent of Gandhi's commitment to his people and his ideas, and you don't have to be Indian to applaud that.*'
Tom Hutchinson, The Mail on Sunday.

'Gandhi *seems certain to earn great popular and commercial success. It is a major contribution to a year of thrilling success for British films. Much more important, it is an artist's personal tribute, deeply felt and simply expressed, to the spiritual worth of another human being.*'
David Robinson, The Times

Edward Fox as General Dyer

John Gielgud as Lord Irwin

Trevor Howard as Judge Broomfield

John Mills as the Viceroy

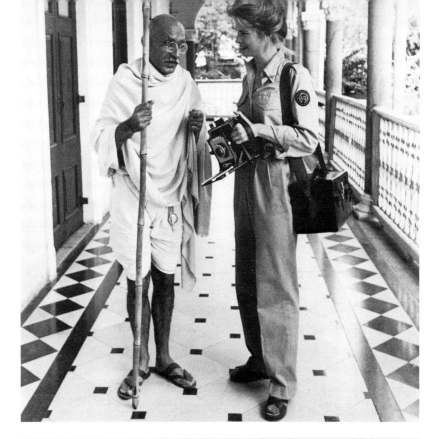

Gandhi with American photojournalist Margaret Bourke-White, played by Candice Bergen.

'There are very few movies that absolutely must be seen. Sir Richard Attenborough's Gandhi is one of them. The British actor-producer-director has dreamed and schemed to make a film about India's greatest political and spiritual leader for 20 years and that's more than enough time for such a vast project to curdle and die. But Attenborough persevered, and it's hard to decide which is more miraculous, the fact that he's actually made the film or the fact that it's turned out so fresh, so electric, so moving.'
Jack Kroll, Newsweek.

Gandhi confers with Mahadev Desai (Pankaj Mohan), Mirabehn (Geraldine James), Jinnah (Aleque Padamsee), Pyarelal (Pankaj Kapoor), Sardar Patel (Saeed Jaffrey), Maulana Azad (Virendra Razdan), Pandit Nehru (Roshan Seth) and Kripalani (Anang Desai) at the ashram.

'Gandhi *is this decade's* Lawrence of Arabia, *a visually magnificent, historically sweeping film that succeeds in capturing the humanity of its magnetic central figure. Ben Kingsley's astonishing performance, capturing both Gandhi's divine light and his irresistible simplicity, inspires this ambitious film.'*
People Magazine, USA.

LEFT
The young Gandhi escorts Walker, an American journalist played by Martin Sheen, around his first ashram in South Africa.

ABOVE
In middle age Gandhi is taught to spin by his wife Kasturba, played by Rohini Hattangady.

TOP RIGHT
The first encounter between Gandhi and the Reverend Charlie Andrews, played by Ian Charleson, takes place in South Africa.

LEFT
Accompanied by Mirabehn, played by Geraldine James, and Charlie, Gandhi greets well wishers in London's East End.

RIGHT
Under orders from General Dyer, troops fire on a crowd trapped in the Jallianwalla Bagh at Amritsar. In less than fifteen minutes they discharge 1650 rounds causing 1515 casualties and fatalities.

'Gandhi is a remarkable feat. And an ironic one. After a line of Englishmen, who for half a century tried to silence the living Gandhi, another Englishman has enabled the dead Mahatma to speak to the whole earth.' Rajmohan Gandhi (Mahatma Gandhi's grandson) *Statesman*, Calcutta.

'Gandhi is the kind of massive accomplishment for which ordinary adjectives like "brilliant" or "sweeping" or "magnificent" seem anemic and inadequate. It is simply the movie of the year . . . No person who cares about what greatness the movie screen is capable of should miss it.' *Rex Reed*, New York Post.

BELOW
South African mounted police charge protesting miners led by Gandhi.

'At the centre of this week's major movie is a small, bald, bespectacled figure who has walked with crowds and kept his virtue and talked with kings without losing the common touch, an astute politician with a steely sense of destiny, yet renowned for his modesty and revered by his followers as an almost saintly person. He is, of course, Sir Richard Attenborough . . .'
Philip French, The Observer.

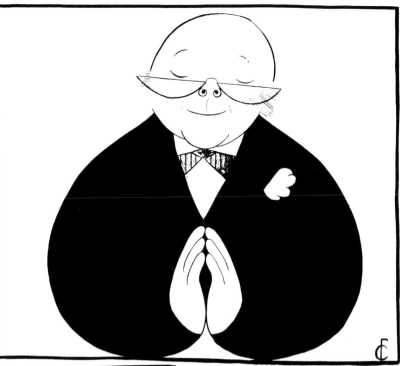

'An excellent biographical subject is treated here with the respect and attention that it deserves and with the impartiality that time and the film maker's intelligence have made possible. A paradox in himself and a creator of paradoxes, Gandhiji steps forth from these vivid frames with all the force of legend and all the human detail and frailty of a real person made more real by circumstances. This is made possible by Ben Kingsley's extraordinary performance; it is inspired acting of the highest order.'
K. M. Amladi, The Times of India.

'The credit goes beyond the performance and the spectacle, the drama and the history, the texture and the visual glories. It goes to the intelligence, the taste and perceptions of Richard Attenborough, who has indeed come a long way from his acting debut as the 19-year-old seaman in In Which We Serve.'
Judith Crist, 50 Plus.

Filmography

The dates used here refer to the first year of public showing

1942   IN WHICH WE SERVE

Producer: Noël Coward
Associate Producer: Anthony Havelock-Allan
Directed by: Noël Coward and David Lean
Photographed by: Ronald Neame
Script: Noël Coward
Music: Noël Coward

Cast: Noël Coward, John Mills, Bernard Miles, Celia Johnson, Joyce Carey, Kay Walsh, Michael Wilding, Kathleen Harrison, RA.

1943   SCHWEIK'S NEW ADVENTURES

Written and Directed by: Karel Lamek
Associate Producer: Walter Sors
Music: Clifton Parker
Musical Director: Muir Matheson

Cast: Lloyd Pearson, George Carney, Julien Mitchell, RA, Margaret McGrath.

1944   THE HUNDRED POUND WINDOW

Directed by: Brian Desmond Hurst
Screenplay by: Abem Finkel
Adaption: Brock Williams
Additional dialogue: Rodney Ackland
Music: Hans May

Cast: Anne Crawford, David Farrar, Frederick Leister, Mary Clare, RA.

1945   JOURNEY TOGETHER

Director: John Boulting
Story: Terence Rattigan
Production Manager & 2nd Unit Supervisor: George Brown
Director of Photography: Harry Waxman, BSC, FRPS
Production Designer: John Howell
Supervising Editor: Reginald Beck
Music: Gordon Jacob

Cast: Edward G. Robinson, RA, Bessie Love, Ronald Squire, Jack Watling, David Tomlinson, John Justin, George Cole, Miles Malleson.

1946   A MATTER OF LIFE AND DEATH
(*Stairway to Heaven* in USA)

Producers/Directors/Scenarists: Michael Powell & Emeric Pressburger
Lighting Cameraman: Jack Cardiff
Camera Operator: Geoffrey Unsworth
Art Director: Alfred Junge
Music: Allan Gray

Cast: David Niven, Roger Livesey, Raymond Massey, Kim Hunter, Marius Goring, Robert Coote, Kathleen Byron, Bonar Colleano, RA.

1946   SCHOOL FOR SECRETS

Producers: Peter Ustinov, George H. Brown
Director: Peter Ustinov

Written by: Peter Ustinov
Director of Photography: Jack Hildyard

Cast: Ralph Richardson, Raymond Huntley, RA, Marjorie Rhodes, John Laurie, David Tomlinson, Ernest Jay, David Hutcheson, Patrick Waddington, Finlay Currie, Michael Hordern, Pamela Matthews.

1947   THE MAN WITHIN
(*The Smugglers* in USA)

Producers: Muriel & Sydney Box
Director: Bernard Knowles
From the novel by: Graham Greene
Script: Muriel & Sydney Box
Photography: Geoffrey Unsworth, BSC
Score: Muir Matheson

Cast: Michael Redgrave, Jean Kent, Joan Greenwood, RA, Francis L. Sullivan, Felix Aylmer, Ronald Shiner, Ernest Thesiger, Basil Sydney.

1947   DANCING WITH CRIME

Producer: James Carter
Director: John Paddy Carstairs
Screenplay: Brock Williams

Cast: RA, Barry K. Barnes, Sheila Sim, Garry Marsh, John Warwick, Judy Kelly, Barry Jones, and Bill Rowbotham (later known as Bill Owen).

1948   BRIGHTON ROCK

Producer: Roy Boulting
Director: John Boulting
Associate Producer: Peter de Sarigny
Screenplay: Graham Greene & Terence Rattigan
Director of Photography: Harry Waxman, BSC, FRPS
Music: Hans May

Cast: RA, Hermione Baddeley, William Hartnell, Carol Marsh, Nigel Stock, Wylie Watson, Harcourt Williams, Charles Goldner, George Carney.

1948   LONDON BELONGS TO ME

Producers: Frank Launder & Sidney Gilliat
Director: Sidney Gilliat
Screenplay: Sidney Gilliat & J. B. Williams
From the novel by: Norman Collins
Director of Photography: Wilkie Cooper
Music: Benjamin Frankel
Conducted by: Muir Matheson

Cast: RA, Alastair Sim, Fay Compton, Stephen Murray, Wylie Watson, Susan Shaw, Maurice Denham.

1948   THE GUINEA PIG

Producer: John Boulting
Director: Roy Boulting
Associate Producer: Peter de Sarigny
Screenplay: Bernard Miles & Warren Chetham Strode in association with Roy Boulting
Director of Photography: Gilbert Taylor
Art Director: John Howell

Production Manager: John Palmer
Editor: Richard Best
Camera Operator: Skeets Kelly
Continuity: Angela Martelli
Music: John Wooldridge
The Saintbury School Song & Dance numbers by: John Addison

Cast: RA, Sheila Sim, Bernard Miles, Cecil Trouncer, Robert Flemyng, Edith Sharpe, Joan Hickson.

1949   THE LOST PEOPLE

Producer: Gordon Wellesley
Director: Bernard Knowles
Screenplay: Bridget Boland (based on her play *Cockpit*)
Director of Photography: Jack Asher
Music: John Greenwood
Music Director: Muir Matheson

Cast: Dennis Price, Mai Zetterling, RA, Siobhan McKenna, Maxwell Reed, William Hartnell.

1950   BOYS IN BROWN

Producer: Anthony Darnborough
Director: Montgomery Tully
Based on the play by: Reginald Beckwith
Screenplay: Montgomery Tully
Directors of Photography: Gordon Lang & Cyril Bristow

Cast: Jack Warner, RA, Dirk Bogarde, Jimmy Hanley, Barbara Murray, Patrick Holt, Andrew Crawford, Thora Hird, Graham Payn, Michael Medwin, Alfie Bass.

1950   MORNING DEPARTURE

Producer: Jay Lewis
Administrator: Leslie Parkyn
Director: Roy Baker
Screenplay: W. E. C. Fairchild
Director of Photography: Desmond Dickinson
Art Director: Alex Vetchinsky

Cast: John Mills, RA, Nigel Patrick, Lana Morris, Peter Hammond, Helen Cherry, James Hayter, Andrew Crawford, George Cole, Victor Maddern, Bernard Lee, Kenneth More, Zena Marshall.

1951   HELL IS SOLD OUT

Producer: Raymond Stross
Director: Michael Anderson
Script: Guy Morgan & Moie Charles
Photography: Jack Asher

Cast: RA, Mai Zetterling, Herbert Lom, Kathleen Byron, Hermione Baddeley.

1951   THE MAGIC BOX

Producer: Ronald Neame
Director: John Boulting
Screenplay: Eric Ambler
Lighting Cameraman: Jack Cardiff
Production Designer: John Bryan
Editor: Richard Best
Music: William Alwyn

Cast: Robert Donat, Renée Asherson, RA, Robert Beatty, Michael Dennison, Henry Edwards, Leo Genn, Marius Goring, Joyce Grenfell, Robertson Hare, Kathleen Harrison, William Hartnell, Stanley Holloway, John Howard Davies, Jack Hulbert, Glynis Johns,

Mervyn Johns, Margaret Johnston, Barry Jones, Miles Malleson, Muir Matheson, A. E. Matthews, John McCallum, Bernard Miles, Laurence Olivier, Cecil Parker, Eric Portman, Dennis Price, Michael Redgrave, Margaret Rutherford, Maria Schell, Ronald Shiner, Sheila Sim, Basil Sydney, Sybil Thorndike, David Tomlinson, Cecil Trouncer, Peter Ustinov, Frederick Valk, Kay Walsh, Emlyn Williams, Harcourt Williams, Googie Withers.

1952   GIFT HORSE

Director: Compton Bennett
In Charge of Production: George Pitcher
Screenplay: Bill Fairchild, Hugh Hastings, William Rose
Director of Photography: Harry Waxman, BSC, FRPS
Editor: Alan Osbiston
Production Manager: Jack Rix
Music: Clifton Parker

Cast: Trevor Howard, RA, Sonny Tufts, James Donald, Joan Rice, Bernard Lee, Dora Bryan, Sidney James.

1953   FATHER'S DOING FINE

Producer: Victor Skutezky
Director: Henry Cass
From the comedy *Little Lambs Eat Ivy* by: Noel Langley
Screenplay: Anne Burnaby
Director of Photography: Erwin Hillier
Art Director: Don Ashton

Cast: RA, Heather Thatcher, Peter Hammond, Susan Stephen, George Thorpe, Virginia McKenna, Jack Watling, Noel Purcell, Mary Germaine, Brian Worth, Diane Hart, Ambrosine Phillpotts

1954   EIGHT O'CLOCK WALK

Producer: George King
Director: Lance Comfort
Screenplay: Katherine Strueby & Guy Morgan
Cinematographer: Brendan Stafford
Music composed & conducted by: George Melachrino

Cast: RA, Cathy O'Donnell, Derek Farr, Ian Hunter, Maurice Denham.

1955   THE SHIP THAT DIED OF SHAME

Producer: Michael Relph
Director: Basil Dearden
Screenplay: Michael Relph, Basil Dearden & John Whiting
From the novel by: Nicholas Montsarrat
Director of Photography: Gordon Dines
Music: William Alwyn

Cast: RA, George Baker, Bill Owen, Virginia McKenna, Roland Culver, Bernard Lee

1956   PRIVATE'S PROGRESS

Producer: Roy Boulting
Director: John Boulting
Director of Photography: Eric Cross
Screenplay: Frank Harvey with John Boulting
Editor: Anthony Harvey
Music composed & directed by: John Addison

Cast: RA, Dennis Price, Terry Thomas, Ian Carmichael, Peter Jones, William Hartnell, Thorley Walters, Jill Adams, Ian Bannen, Victor Maddern, Kenneth Griffith, John le Mesurier, John Warren.

1956 THE BABY AND THE BATTLESHIP

Producer: Anthony Darnborough
Director: Jay Lewis
Screenplay: Jay Lewis, Gilbert Hackforth-Jones
Additional scenes & dialogue: Bryan Forbes
Director of Photography: Harry Waxman, BSC, FRPS
Camera Operator: Ronald Taylor
Art Director: John Howell
Editor: Manuel Del Campo

Cast: John Mills, RA, André Morell, Bryan Forbes, Michael Howard, Lisa Gastoni, Ernest Clark, Harry Locke, Michael Hordern, Lionel Jeffries, Clifford Mollison, Thorley Walters, Kenneth Griffith, John le Mesurier, Gordon Jackson.

1957 BROTHERS IN LAW

Producer: John Boulting
Director: Roy Boulting
Screenplay: Frank Harvey, Jeffrey Dell, Roy Boulting
Director of Photography: Max Greene
Editor: Anthony Harvey
Music composed and directed by: Benjamin Frankel

Cast: RA, Ian Carmichael, Terry Thomas, Jill Adams, Miles Malleson, Raymond Huntley, Eric Barker, Nicholas Parsons, John le Mesurier, Irene Handl, Leslie Phillips, Kenneth Griffith.

1957 THE SCAMP

Producer: James H. Lawrie
Director: Wolf Rilla
Screenplay: Wolf Rilla
Associate Producer: Denis O'Dell
Lighting Cameraman: Freddie Francis
Editor: Bernard Gribble
Musical Director: Francis Chagrin

Cast: RA, Terence Morgan, Colin Petersen, Dorothy Alison, Jill Adams, Geoffrey Keene, Margaretta Scott, Maureen Delany.

1958 DUNKIRK

Producer: Michael Balcon
Director: Leslie Norman
Associate Producer: Michael Forlong
Screenplay: David Divine & W. P. Lipscombe
Production Supervisor: Hal Mason
Director of Photography: Paul Beeson, BSC
Editor: Gordon Stone
Art Director: Jim Morahan
Music: Malcolm Arnold

Cast: John Mills, RA, Bernard Lee, Robert Urquhart, Ray Jackson, Ronald Hines, Sean Barratt, Roland Curram, Meredith Edwards, Patricia Plunkett, Maxine Audley, Lionel Jeffries, Victor Maddern, Flanagan & Allen.

1958 THE MAN UPSTAIRS

Producer: Robert Dunbar
Director: Don Chaffey
Original story & screenplay: Alun Falconer
Production Controller: Ralph Bond
Lighting Cameraman: Gerald Gibbs
Editor: John Trumper

Cast: RA, Bernard Lee, Donald Houston, Dorothy Alison, Virginia Maskell, Charles Houston, Maureen Connell, Kenneth Griffith, Patricia Jessel, Edward Judd, Alfred Burke.

1958 SEA OF SAND

Producers: Robert Baker & Monty Berman
Director: Guy Green
Screenplay: Robert Westerby
Director of Photography: Wilkie Cooper
Editor: Gordon Pilkington
Music: Clifton Parker.

Cast: RA, John Gregson, Michael Craig, Vincent Ball, Percy Herbert, Barry Foster, Andrew Faulds, George Murcell.

1959 DANGER WITHIN

Producer: Colin Leslie
Director: Don Chaffey
Associate Producer: Adrian D. Worker
Screenplay: Bryan Forbes & Frank Harvey
Director of Photography: Arthur Grant
Art Director: Ray Simm
Editor: John Trumper
Music: Francis Chagrin

Cast: Richard Todd, Bernard Lee, Michael Wilding, RA, Dennis Price, Donald Houston, William Franklyn, Vincent Ball, Peter Arne, Peter Jones, Ronnie Stevens, Terence Alexander, Andrew Faulds.

1959 I'M ALL RIGHT JACK

Producer: Roy Boulting
Director: John Boulting
Screenplay: Frank Harvey & John Boulting with Alan Hackney
Production Supervisor: Adrian D. Worker
Director of Photography: Max Greene
Editor: Anthony Harvey
Art Director: Bill Andrews

Cast: Ian Carmichael, Terry Thomas, Peter Sellers, RA, Dennis Price, Margaret Rutherford, Irene Handl, Liz Fraser, Miles Malleson, John le Mesurier, Raymond Huntley, Victor Maddern, Kenneth Griffith, Malcolm Muggeridge, Michael Bates, David Lodge, Harry Locke.

1959 JETSTORM

Producer: Steven Pallos
Director: C. Raker Endfield
Screenplay by: C. Raker Endfield & Sigmund Miller
Director of Photography: Jack Hildyard, BSC
Art Director: Scott MacGregor
Editor: Oswalde Hafenrichter
Music composed and sung by: Marty Wilde

Cast: RA, Stanley Baker, Hermione Baddeley, Bernard Braden, Diane Cilento, Barbara Kelly, David Kossoff, Virginia Maskell, Harry Secombe, Elizabeth Sellars, Sybil Thorndike, Mai Zetterling, Marty Wilde, Patrick Allen, Megs Jenkins, Lance Morris, George Rose.

1959 SOS PACIFIC

Producers: John Nasht & Patrick Filmer-Sankey
Director: Guy Green
Screenplay: Robert Westerby
Cameraman: Wilkie Cooper
Art Director: George Provis
Music: Georges Auric

Cast: RA, Pier Angeli, John Gregson, Eva Bartok, Eddie Constantine, Jean Anderson, Clifford Evans.

1960 THE ANGRY SILENCE

Producers: RA & Bryan Forbes
Director: Guy Green
Associate Producer: Jack Rix
Written by: Bryan Forbes
Photographed by: Arthur Ibbetson, BSC
Editor: Anthony Harvey
Art Director: Ray Simm
Music composed and conducted by: Malcolm Arnold

Cast: RA, Pier Angeli, Michael Craig, Bernard Lee, Alfred Burke, Geoffrey Keen, Laurence Naismith, Penelope Horner, Norman Bird, Gerald Sim, Brian Bedford, Brian Murray, Oliver Reed.

1960 THE LEAGUE OF GENTLEMEN

Producer: Michael Relph
Director: Basil Dearden
Screenplay: Bryan Forbes
Based on the novel by: John Boland
Director of Photography: Arthur Ibbetson, BSC
Art Director: Peter Proud
Editor: John Gutheridge
Music composed & directed by: Philip Green

Cast: Jack Hawkins, RA, Roger Livesey, Nigel Patrick, Bryan Forbes, Kieron Moore, Robert Coote, Terence Alexander, Melissa Stribling, Norman Bird, Nanette Newman, David Lodge, Patrick Wymark, Lydia Sherwood, Doris Hare, Gerald Harper, Brian Murray.

1961 WHISTLE DOWN THE WIND

Producer: RA
Director: Bryan Forbes
Screenplay: Keith Waterhouse & Willis Hall
From the original novel by: Mary Hayley Bell
Associate Producer: Jack Rix
Lighting Cameraman: Arthur Ibbetson, BSC
Art Director: Ray Simm
Editor: Max Benedict
Music composed and conducted by: Malcolm Arnold

Cast: Hayley Mills, Bernard Lee, Alan Bates, Norman Bird, Elsie Wagstaff, Ronald Hines, Gerald Sim, Diane Holgate, Alan Barnes, Roy Holder.

1962 ONLY TWO CAN PLAY

Producer: Leslie Gilliat
Director: Sidney Gilliat
Screenplay: Bryan Forbes
From the novel *That Uncertain Feeling* by: Kingsley Amis
Director of Photography: John Wilcox
Art Director: Albert Witherick
Editor: Thelma Connell
Music: Richard Rodney Bennett

Cast: Peter Sellers, Mai Zetterling, Virginia Maskell, RA, Kenneth Griffith, Raymond Huntley, John le Mesurier, Graham Stark.

1962 THE L-SHAPED ROOM

Producers: James Woolf & RA
Written for the screen & directed by: Bryan Forbes
Based on the novel by: Lynne Reid Banks
Director of Photography: Douglas Slocombe
Art Director: Ray Simm
Editor: Anthony Harvey
Music from Brahms' First Piano Concerto
Jazz Sequence: John Barry

Cast: Leslie Caron, Tom Bell, Cicely Courtnedge,
Bernard Lee, Brock Peters, Nanette Newman, Patricia Phoenix, Emlyn Williams, Avis Bunnage, Gerald Sim, Harry Locke, Mark Eden, Pamela Sholto.

1962 ALL NIGHT LONG

Executive Producer: Bob Roberts
Producer: Michael Relph
Director: Basil Dearden
Original Screenplay: Nel King & Peter Achilles
Director of Photography: Ted Scaife, BSC
Art Director: Ray Simm
Editor: John Guthridge
Musical Director: Philip Green.

Cast: Patrick McGoohan, RA, Marti Stevens, Betsy Blair, Keith Michell, Paul Harris, Bernard Braden, and, as themselves, Dave Brubeck, Johnny Dankworth, Charles Mingus, Tubby Hayes.

1962 THE DOCK BRIEF
(*Trial and Error* in USA)

Producer: Dimitri de Grunwald
Associate Producer: John Mortimer
Director: James Hill
Screenplay: Pierre Rouve
Photographed by: Ted Scaife, BSC
Art Director: Ray Simm
Editor: Ann Chegwidden
Make-Up: Tom Smith
Music: Ron Grainer

Cast: Peter Sellers, RA, Beryl Reid, David Lodge.

1963 THE GREAT ESCAPE

Producer/Director: John Sturges
Screenplay: James Clavell & W. R. Burnett
Based on the book by: Paul Brickhill
Cinematographer: Daniel Fapp
Art Director: Fernando Carrère
Editor: Ferris Webster
Music: Elmer Bernstein

Cast: Steve McQueen, James Garner, RA, James Donald, Charles Bronson, Donald Pleasance, James Coburn, John Leyton, Gordon Jackson, David McCallum, Nigel Stock, Hans Messemer, William Russell, Angus Lennie, Jud Taylor.

1964 SEANCE ON A WET AFTERNOON

Producer: RA
Written & directed by: Bryan Forbes
From the novel by: Mark McShane
Associate Producer: Jack Rix
Photographed by: Gerry Turpin
Art Director: Ray Simm
Editor: Derek York
Make-up: Stuart Freeborn
Music composed, arranged and conducted by: John Barry

Cast: Kim Stanley, RA, Nanette Newman, Patrick McGee, Mark Eden, Gerald Sim, Marian Spencer, Judith Donner, Ronald Hines.

1964 THE THIRD SECRET

Producer: Robert L. Joseph
Director: Charles Crichton
Screenplay by: Robert L. Joseph
Associate Producer: Shirley Bernstein
Director of Photography: Douglas Slocombe
Production Designer: Tom Morahan

Editor: Frederick Wilson
Music composed & conducted by: Richard Arnell

Cast: Stephen Boyd, Jack Hawkins, RA, Diane Cilento, Pamela Franklin, Paul Rogers, Alan Webb, Rachel Kempson, Peter Sallis, Patience Collier, Freda Jackson, Judi Dench, Peter Copley, Nigel Davenport.

1964 GUNS AT BATASI

Producer: George H. Brown
Director: John Guillermin
Screenplay: Robert Holles
Based on his novel *The Siege of Battersea*
Director of Photography: Douglas Slocombe
Art Director: Maurice Carter
Editor: Max Benedict
Music composed & conducted by: John Addison

Cast: RA, Flora Robson, John Leyton, Jack Hawkins, Mia Farrow, Cecil Parker, Errol John, Graham Stark, Earl Cameron, Percy Herbert, David Lodge, Bernard Horsfall, John Meillon.

1966 THE FLIGHT OF THE PHOENIX

Producer/Director: Robert Aldrich
Associate Producer: Walter Blake
Screenplay: Lukas Heller
From the novel by: Elleston Trevor
Director of Photography: Joseph Biroc, ASC
Art Director: William Glasgow
Editor: Michael Luciano, ACE
Aerial Sequences: Paul Mantz
Music: De Vol

Cast: James Stewart, RA, Peter Finch, Hardy Kruger, Ernest Borgnine, Ian Bannen, Ronald Fraser, Christian Marquand, Dan Duryea, George Kennedy.

1967 THE SAND PEBBLES

Producer/Director: Robert Wise
Associate Producer and Second Unit Director: Charles Maguire
Screenplay: Robert Anderson
From the Novel by: Richard McKenna
Director of Photography: Joseph MacDonald, ASC
Production Designer: Boris Leven
Editor: William Reynolds, ACE

Cast: Steve McQueen, RA, Richard Crenna, Candice Bergen, Marayat Andriane, Mako, Larry Gates, Charles Robinson.

1967 DR DOLITTLE

Producer: Arthur P. Jacobs
Associate Producer: Mort Abrahams
Director: Richard Fleischer
Screenplay: Leslie Bricusse
Based on the Doctor Dolittle stories by: Hugh Lofting
Director of Photography: Robert Surtees, ASC
Production Designer: Mario Chiari
Editors: Samuel E. Beetley, ACE, Marjorie Fowler, ACE
Music and lyrics by: Leslie Bricusse
Dance and musical numbers staged by: Herbert Ross

Cast: Rex Harrison, Samantha Eggar, Anthony Newley, RA.

1968 ONLY WHEN I LARF

Producers: Len Deighton & Brian Duffy
Director: Basil Dearden
Screenplay: John Salmon

Photography: Anthony Richmond
Art Director: John Blezard
Editor: Fergus McDonell
Music: Ron Grainer

Cast: RA, David Hemmings, Alexandra Stewart, Nicholas Pennell, Melissa Stribling, Terence Alexander.

1968 THE BLISS OF MRS BLOSSOM

Producer: Josef Shaftel
Director: Joseph McGrath
Screenplay: Alec Coppel & Denis Norden
Director of Photography: Geoffrey Unsworth, BSC
Production Designer: Assheton Gorton
Editor: Ralph Sheldon
Music: Riz Ortolani

Cast: Shirley MacLaine, RA, James Booth, Freddie Jones, William Ruston, Bob Monkhouse, Patricia Routledge.

1969 OH! WHAT A LOVELY WAR[1]

Producers: Brian Duffy & RA
Director: RA[1]
Associate Producer: Mack Davidson
Director of Photography: Gerry Turpin[2]
Production Designer: Don Ashton[2]
Songs orchestrated and incidental music composed and conducted by: Alfred Ralston
Costume Designer: Anthony Mendelson[2]
Choreography: Eleanor Fazan
Editor: Kevin Connor[1]
Assistant Director: Claude Watson
Camera Operator: Ronnie Taylor
Continuity: Ann Skinner
Production Manager: John Comfort
Sound Mixer: Simon Kaye[2]
Music Editor: Michael Clifford
Sound Editors: Don Challis[2] and Brian Holland
Dubbing Mixer: Gerry Humphreys
Art Director: Harry White
Set Dresser: Peter James
Casting: Miriam Brickman
Make-up Supervisor: Stuart Freeborn
Chief Hairdresser: Biddy Chrystal
Boom Operator: Tom Buchanan
Special Effects: Ron Ballanger
Location Manager: Bryan Coates

[1] *British Academy of Film and Television Arts Nomination for award.*
[2] *British Academy of Film and Television Arts Award.*

Cast: Dirk Bogarde, Phyllis Calvert, Jean Pierre Cassel, John Clements, John Gielgud, Jack Hawkins, John Mills, Kenneth More, Laurence Olivier,[2] Michael Redgrave, Vanessa Redgrave, Ralph Richardson, Maggie Smith, Susannah York, Meriel Forbes, Ian Holm, Paul Daneman, Joe Melia, Kim Smith, Mary Wimbush,[1] Paul Shelley, Wendy Allnutt, John Rae, Kathleen Wileman, Corin Redgrave, Malcolm McFee, Colin Farrell, Maurice Roeves, Angela Thorne, David Lodge, Peter Gilmore, Derek Newark, Ron Pember, Juliet Mills, Nanette Newman, Cecil Parker, Robert Flemyng, Thorley Walters, Isabel Dean, Guy Middleton, Natasha Parry, Edward Fox, Clifford Mollison, Harry Locke, Michael Bates, Pia Colombo, Vincent Ball, Anthony Ainley, Gerald Sim, Maurice Arthur, Marianne Stone, Charlotte Attenborough.

1969 THE MAGIC CHRISTIAN

Executive Producers: Henry T. Weinstein, Anthony B. Unger
Producer: Denis O'Dell
Director: Joseph McGrath
Screenplay: Terry Southern, Joseph McGrath, Peter Sellers
Based on the novel by: Terry Southern
Additional Material: Graham Chapman, John Cleese
Photography: Geoffrey Unsworth, BSC
Production Designer: Assheton Gorton
Editor: Kevin Connor

Cast: Peter Sellers, Ringo Starr, RA, Laurence Harvey, Christopher Lee, Spike Milligan, Yul Brynner, Roman Polanski, Raquel Welch, Isabel Jeans, Wilfred Hyde-White, Terence Alexander, Patrick Cargill, Clive Dunn, Fred Emney, Peter Graves, Patrick Holt, Hattie Jacques, John le Mesurier, Ferdy Mayne, Guy Middleton, Dennis Price, Graham Stark, Edward Underdown, Michael Aspel, Michael Barratt, Harry Carpenter, W. Barrington Dalby, John Snagge, Alan Whicker.

1970 THE LAST GRENADE

Producer: Josef Shaftel
Director: Gordon Flemyng
Screenplay: Kenneth Ware
Director of Photography: Alan Hume BSC
Art Director: Anthony Pratt
Editors: Ernest Hosler & Ann Chegwidden
Music composed and conducted by: John Dankworth

Cast: Stanley Baker, Alex Cord, Honor Blackman, RA, Ray Brooks, John Thaw, Gerald Sim

1970 DAVID COPPERFIELD

Producer: Frederick Brogger
Director: Delbert Mann
Screenplay: Jack Pulman
Based on the novel by: Charles Dickens
Director of Photography: Ken Hodges, BSC
Art Director: Alex Vetchinsky
Editor: Peter Boita
Music composed and conducted by: Malcolm Arnold.

Cast: RA, Cyril Cusack, Edith Evans, Pamela Franklin, Susan Hampshire, Wendy Hiller, Ron Moody, Laurence Olivier, Robin Phillips, Michael Redgrave, Ralph Richardson, Emlyn Williams, Sinead Cusack, James Donald, James Hayter, Megs Jenkins, Anna Massey, Corin Redgrave.

1970 LOOT

Producer: Arthur Lewis
Director: Silvio Narizzano
Based on the play by: Joe Orton
Screenplay: Ray Galton & Alan Simpson
Art Director: Anthony Pratt
Lighting Cameraman: Austin Dempster
Editor: Martin Charles

Cast: RA, Lee Remick, Hywel Bennett, Milo O'Shea, Roy Holder, Dick Emery.

1971 A SEVERED HEAD

Producer: Elliott Kastner
Co-Producer: Alan Ladd, Jr.
Director: Dick Clement
Screenplay: Frederic Raphael

Lighting Cameraman: Austin Dempster
Production Designer: Richard MacDonald
Editor: Peter Hatherley

Cast: Lee Remick, RA, Ian Holm, Claire Bloom, Jennie Linden, Clive Revill.

1971 10 RILLINGTON PLACE

Producers: Martin Ransohoff & Leslie Linder
Director: Richard Fleischer
Associate Producer: Basil Appleby
Screenplay: Clive Exton
Based on the book by: Ludovic Kennedy
Director of Photography: Denys Coop BSC
Art Director: Maurice Carter
Editor: Ernest Walter
Makeup: Stuart Freeborn
Music: John Dankworth

Cast: RA, Judy Geeson, John Hurt, Pat Heywood, André Morell, Robert Hardy, Geoffrey Chater, Basil Dignam.

1972 YOUNG WINSTON

Producer/Writer: Carl Foreman[3]
Director: RA
Associate Producer: Harold Buck
Production Supervisors: Michael Stanley-Evans, Sidney G. Barnsby
Director of Photography: Gerry Turpin, BSC
Production Designers: Don Ashton[1,3], Geoffrey Drake[3]
Music: Alfred Ralston[1]
Costume Designer: Anthony Mendelson[2,3]
Editor: Kevin Connor
Camera Operator: Ronnie Taylor
Assistant Director: William P. Cartlidge
Sound Mixer: Simon Kaye
Continuity: Ann Skinner
Art Directors: John Graysmark[3] and Bill Hutchinson[3]
Set Dresser: Peter James[3]
Make-up Supervisor: Stuart Freeborn
Chief Hairdresser: Biddy Chrystal
Casting: Miriam Brickman
Dubbing Editor: Jonathan Bates
Sound Boom Operator: Tom Buchanan
Special Effects: Cliff Richardson, Tom Howard and Charles Staffel

Cast: Robert Shaw,[1] Anne Bancroft,[1] Simon Ward,[1] John Mills, Jack Hawkins, Ian Holm, Anthony Hopkins, Patrick Magee, Edward Woodward, Raymond Huntley, Russell Lewis, Pat Heywood, Laurence Naismith, Basil Dignam, Robert Hardy, Colin Blakely, Noel Davis, Michael Audreson, Richard Leech, Clive Morton, Robert Flemyng, Jeremy Child, Jane Seymour, Dinsdale Landen, Julian Holloway, Thorley Walters, Patrick Holt, Norman Bird, Gerald Sim, Andrew Faulds, Maurice Roeves, Nigel Hawthorne, James Cossins, John Woodvine, Norman Rossington, George Mikell, Pippa Steel, Norman Gay, Robert Harris.

[1] *British Academy of Film and Television Arts Nomination for award.*
[2] *British Academy of Film and Television Arts Award.*
[3] *Academy of Motion Picture Arts and Sciences Nomination for Award.*

1975 ROSEBUD

Producer/Director: Otto Preminger
Screenplay: Erik Lee Preminger
Director of Photography: Denys Coop, BSC
Production Designer: Michael Seymour
Editors: Peter Thornton and Tom Noble

Cast: Peter O'Toole, RA, Cliff Gorman, Claude
Dauphin, John V. Lindsay, Peter Lawford, Raf Vallone,
Adrienne Corri, Lalla Ward.

1975 BRANNIGAN

Executive Producer: Michael Wayne
Producer: Arthur Gardner & Jules Levy
Director: Douglas Hickox
Screenplay: Christopher Trumbo, Michael Butler,
William McGivern, William Norton.
Story: Christopher Trumbo & Michael Butler.
Lighting Cameraman: Gerry Fisher
Art Director: Ted Marshall
Editor: Malcolm Cooke

Cast: John Wayne, RA, Judy Geeson, Mel Ferrer, John
Vernon, Leslie Ann Down, John Stride, James Booth.

1975 CONDUCT UNBECOMING

Producers: Michael Deeley, Barry Spikings
Co-Producer: Andrew Donally
Director: Michael Anderson
Screenplay: Robert Enders
Director of Photography: Bob Huke BSC
Art Director: Ted Tester
Film Editor: John Glen
Make Up: Tom Smith

Cast: Michael York, RA, Trevor Howard, Stacy Keach,
Christopher Plummer, Susannah York, James Faulkner,
Michael Culver, James Donald, Helen Cherry.

1975 AND THEN THERE WERE NONE
(*Ten Little Indians* in USA)

Producer: Harry Alan Towers
Director: Peter Collinson
Screenplay: Peter Welbeck
From the novel by: Agatha Christie
Photography by: Fernando Arribas
Editor: John Trumper
Music: Bruno Nicholai

Cast: Oliver Reed, RA, Elke Sommer, Herbert Lom,
Gert Froebe, Stephane Audran, Charles Aznavour,
Adolfo Celi.

1977 A BRIDGE TOO FAR[1]

Producers: Joseph E. Levine & Richard P. Levine
Director: RA[1]
Co-Producer: Michael Stanley-Evans
Screenplay: William Goldman
Director of Photography: Geoffrey Unsworth BSC[2]
Production Designer: Terence Marsh[1]
Editor: Antony Gibbs[1]
Music composed & conducted by: John Addison[2]
Associate Producer: John Palmer
Production Supervisor: Eric Rattray
Camera Operator: Peter MacDonald
Sound Recordist: Simon Kaye[2]
Production Manager: Terence A. Clegg
Costume Designer: Anthony Mendelson
First Assistant Director: David Tomblin
Special Effects Supervisor: John Richardson

Art Directors: Stuart Craig, Alan Tomkins, Roy
Stannard
Set Dresser: Peter Howitt
Sketch Artist: Michael White
Make-up Supervisor: Tom Smith
Chief Hairdresser: Ronnie Cogan
Continuity: Connie Willis
Aerial Photography: Robin Browne
Casting: Miriam Brickman
Dubbing Mixers: Gerry Humphreys,[2] Robin
O'Donoghue[2]
Sound Editors: Les Wiggins,[2] Peter Horrocks[2]
Sound Boom Operator: David Stephenson
2nd Unit Director: Sidney Hayers
2nd Unit Lighting Cameraman: Harry Waxman

Cast: Dirk Bogarde, James Caan, Michael Caine, Sean
Connery, Edward Fox,[2] Elliott Gould, Gene Hackman,
Anthony Hopkins, Hardy Kruger, Laurence Olivier,
Ryan O'Neal, Robert Redford, Maximilian Schell, Liv
Ullman, Eric Van't Wout, Wolfgang Preiss, Hans Von
Borsody, Peter Faber, Frank Grimes, Jeremy Kemp,
Donald Pickering, Donald Douglas, Stephen Moore,
Michael Byrne, Paul Copley, Gerald Sim, Colin Farrell,
Christopher Good, Alun Armstrong, Anthony Milner,
Barry McCarthy, Keith Drinkel, Mary Smithuysen, Ben
Cross, David English, Ben Howard, Denholm Elliott,
Arthur Hill, John Salthouse, Stanley Lebor, Richard
Kane, John Ratzenberger, Patrick Ryecart, John Stride.

1978 THE CHESS PLAYERS

Producer: Suresh Jindal
Director: Satyajit Ray
Production Executive: Anil Chowdhury
Camera: Soumendu Roy
Art Director: Bansi Chandragupta
Editor: Dulal Dutta
Costumes: Shama Zaidi
Music: Satyajit Ray

Cast: Sanjeev Kumar, Saeed Jaffrey, RA, Amjad Khan,
Shabana Azmi, Farida Jalal, Victor Bannerji, Amitabh
Bachchan (Narrator).

1978 MAGIC

Producers: Joseph E. Levine & Richard P. Levine
Director: RA
Screenplay, based on his novel: William Goldman
Executive Producer: C. O. Erickson
Director of Photography: Victor J. Kemper, ASC
Production Designer: Terence Marsh
Editor: John Bloom
Music: Jerry Goldsmith
First Assistant Director: Arne Schmidt
Art Director: Richard Lawrence
Set Decorator: John Franco, Jr.
Costumes: Ruth Myers
Script Consultant: Ann Skinner
Assistant to Director: Michael White
Casting: Mike Fenton & Jane Feinberg
Sound Mixer: Larry Jost

[1] *British Academy of Film and Television Arts
Nomination for award.*
[2] *British Academy of Film and Television Arts Award.*

Sound Boom: Clint Althouse
Sound Editor: Jonathan Bates
Dubbing Mixers: Gerry Humphreys & Robin
O'Donoghue
Camera Operator: Robert Thomas
Special Effects: Robert MacDonald, Jr.
Makeup Artists: Lee Harman, Hallie Smith-Simmons
Hair Styles: Cherie

Cast: Anthony Hopkins[1], Ann-Margret, Burgess
Meredith, Ed Lauter

1980 THE HUMAN FACTOR

Producer/Director: Otto Preminger
Based on the novel by: Graham Greene
Screenplay: Tom Stoppard
Director of Photography: Mike Molloy
Art Director: Ken Ryan
Editor: Richard Trevor
Music: Richard & Gary Logan

Cast: Nicol Williamson, RA, Derek Jacobi, Robert
Morley, John Gielgud, Ann Todd, Richard Vernon,
Joop Doderer, Iman, Angela Thorne, Paul Curran,
Fiona Fullerton, Adrienne Corri, Marianne Stone.

1982 GANDHI[2,4]

Producer/Director: RA[2,4]
Written by: John Briley[1,4]
Executive Producer: Michael Stanley-Evans
Directors of Photography: Billy Williams BSC[1,4], Ronnie
Taylor BSC[1,4]
Music: Ravi Shankar[1,3]
Orchestral Score and Additional Music: George
Fenton[1,3]
Co-Producer: Rani Dube
In Charge of Production: Terence A. Clegg
Film Editor: John Bloom[1,4]
Production Designer: Stuart Craig[1,4]
Costume Designers: John Mollo[1,4], Bhanu Athaiya[1,4]
Second Unit Director/Cameraman: Govind Nihalani
Sound Recordist: Simon Kaye[1,3]
Associate Producer: Suresh Jindal
Production Managers: Alexander de Grunwald, Shama
Habibullah
First Assistant Director: David Tomblin
Make-Up Supervisor: Tom Smith[1,3]
Chief Hairdresser: Paula Gillespie
Continuity/Script Supervisor: June Randall
Casting Director: Susie Figgis
Assistant to the Director: Michael White
Supervising Art Director: Bob Laing[4]
Art Directors: Ram Yedekar, Norman Dorme
Construction Manager: Dick Frift
Set Decorator: Michael Sierton[4]
Set Dressers: Jill Quertier, Nissar Allana, Amal Allana,
Aruna Harprasad
Camera Operator: Chic Anstiss
Aerial Photographer: Robin Browne
Sound Editor: Jonathan Bates[1,3]
Assembly Editor: Chris Ridsdale
Dubbing Mixers: Gerry Humphreys,[1,3] Robin
O'Donoghue[1,3]
Music Recordist: John Richards
Unit Publicity/Indian Casting: Dolly Thakore
Director of Publicity: Diana Hawkins

Cast: Ben Kingsley,[2,2,4] Candice Bergen, Edward Fox,[1]
John Gielgud, Trevor Howard, John Mills, Martin
Sheen, Rohini Hattangady,[2] Ian Charleson, Athol
Fugard, Gunter Maria Halmer, Saeed Jaffrey, Geraldine

James, Alyque Padamsee, Amrish Puri, Roshan Seth,[1]
Ian Bannen, Michael Bryant, John Clements, Richard
Griffiths, Nigel Hawthorne, Bernard Hepton, Michael
Hordern, Shreeram Lagoo, Om Puri, Virendra Razdan,
Richard Vernon, Harsh Nayyar, Peter Harlowe, Anang
Desai, Winston Ntshona, Peter Cartwright, Marius
Weyers, David Gant, Daniel Day Lewis, Avis Bunnage,
John Savident, Christopher Good, David Markham,
Manohar Pitale, Dominic Guard, Bernard Hill, Nana
Palsikar, Gerald Sim, Colin Farrell, James Cossins,
Gurcharan Singh, John Vine, Geoffrey Chater, Ernest
Clark, Habib Tanveer, Pankaj Mohan, Barry John,
Brian Oulton, Bernard Horsfall, Richard Leech, Pankaj
Kapoor, Terrence Hardiman, Jon Croft, William
Hoyland, John Ratzenberger, Jack McKenzie, Tom
Alter, Dilsher Singh, Sekhar Chatterjee.

[1] *British Academy of Film and Television Arts
Nomination for award.*
[2] *British Academy of Film and Television Arts Award.*
[3] *Academy of Motion Picture Arts and Sciences
Nomination for award.*
[4] *Academy of Motion Picture Arts and Sciences Award.*

Index